S0-BOC-576

Creating Keepsakes

THE **Ultimate**

guide to photo

keepsakes

the art of everyday living

VICE PRESIDENT AND EDITOR-IN-CHIEF Sandra Graham Case

EXECUTIVE DIRECTOR OF PUBLICATIONS Cheryl Nodine Gunnells

SENIOR PUBLICATIONS DIRECTOR Susan White Sullivan

SPECIAL PROJECTS DIRECTOR Susan Frantz Wiles

DIRECTOR OF DESIGNER RELATIONS Debra Nettles

SENIOR ART OPERATIONS DIRECTOR Jeff Curtis

ART IMAGING DIRECTOR Mark Hawkins

PUBLISHING SYSTEMS ADMINISTRATOR Becky Riddle

PUBLISHING SYSTEMS ASSISTANTS Clint Hanson, Josh Hyatt, and John Rose

CHIEF OPERATING OFFICER Tom Siebenmorgen

DIRECTOR OF CORPORATE PLANNING AND DEVELOPMENT Laticia Mull Dittrich

VICE PRESIDENT, SALES AND MARKETING Pam Stebbins

DIRECTOR OF SALES AND SERVICES Margaret Reinold

VICE PRESIDENT, OPERATIONS Jim Dittrich

COMPTROLLER, OPERATIONS Rob Thieme

RETAIL CUSTOMER SERVICE MANAGER Stan Raynor

PRINT PRODUCTION MANAGER Fred F. Pruss

© 2006 Leisure Arts, Inc., 5701 Ranch Drive, Little Rock, Arkansas 72223-9633

This product is manufactured under license for PRIMEDIA Special Interest Publications, Inc.—a PRIMEDIA company, publisher of *Creating Keepsakes* Scrapbook Magazine. ©2006. All rights reserved.

All rights reserved. No part of this publication may be reproduced in any form or by any means without permission in writing from the publisher. Printed in the United States of America. The information in this book is presented in good faith; however, no warranty is given nor are results guaranteed. Leisure Arts, *Creating Keepsakes* Scrapbook Magazine, and PRIMEDIA Inc. disclaim any and all liability for untoward results. Not for commercial reproduction.

We have made every effort to ensure that these instructions are accurate and complete. We cannot, however, be responsible for human error, typographical mistakes or variations in individual work.

The designs in this book are protected by copyright; however, you may use the projects as inspiration for your personal use. This right is surpassed when the projects are made by employees or sold commercially.

Library of Congress Control Number: 2006924516
White, Tracy
Creating Keepsakes
"A Leisure Arts Publication"

Softcover ISBN 1-57486-606-0

CREATING Keepsakes
SCRAPBOOK MAGAZINE

FOUNDING EDITOR Lisa Bearnson

EDITOR-IN-CHIEF Tracy White

MANAGING EDITOR, SPECIAL PROJECTS Leslie Miller

MANAGING EDITOR Marianne Madsen

EDITOR-AT-LARGE Jana Lillie

SENIOR WRITERS Denise Pauley, Rachel Thomae

SENIOR EDITOR, SPECIAL PROJECTS Vanessa Hoy

ASSOCIATE EDITORS Brittany Beattie, Jennifer Purdie

ASSOCIATE WRITER Lori Fairbanks

ASSISTANT EDITOR Britney Mellen

COPY EDITOR Kim Sandoval

EDITORIAL ASSISTANTS Joannie McBride, Fred Brewer, Liesl Russell

ART DIRECTOR Brian Tippetts

ASSOCIATE ART DIRECTOR, SPECIAL PROJECTS Erin Bayless

DESIGNER Celeste Rockwood-Jones

PUBLISHER Tony Golden

VICE PRESIDENT, GROUP PUBLISHER David O'Neil

SVP, GROUP PUBLISHING DIRECTOR Scott Wagner

PRIMEDIA

PRIMEDIA, Inc.

CHAIRMAN, CEO & PRESIDENT Dean Nelson

VICE-CHAIRMAN Beverly C. Chell

table of contents

Foreword

I LOVE talking to people about scrapbooking—when they started, why they enjoy it, what fuels their passion.

Though the stories are as different as the crafters who tell them, I hear a few common themes: Scrapbooking is a creative outlet. It gives us the chance—as adults—to get our fingers in the "mud" and play. It's the ultimate way to preserve memories ... the marriage of photos, words and a personal, imaginative touch. And we all agree that we are creating more than scrapbook pages.

We are creating *keepsakes*.

It's only natural, then, that as crafters, as family historians, we'd want to go beyond the borders of our scrapbook pages. To experiment with ways to record milestones and traditions. To turn our vision and style into gifts for those we love. To display our creations, our works of heart, for everyone to see. To stretch our artistic wings.

Maybe you're a seasoned scrapbooker or an expert crafter. You could be someone like me who's dabbled in every conceivable creative outlet. Or perhaps you're picking up photos, patterned paper or paints for the first time, just looking to get started.

Wherever you're coming from, we're all headed in the same direction—turning our desire to create into mementos that friends and family will treasure. And this book will be a great companion along the way.

The featured projects are full of imagination, innovation and life. Some are simple and quick, others more elaborate. Each chapter provides a balance of scrapbooking and crafting, sentimentality and fun.

But what amazes me most is that despite the variety and versatility, again, a common theme runs throughout. Whether the project is a tribute album to a grandparent, an antique quilt display, some photo coasters or a canister for pet treats, it reflects the style and personality of its designer. It was made with love and a sense of importance. It is a keepsake.

I hope this book ignites your spirit of creativity and inspires you to try something new. I hope it helps you brighten a corner of your home with a meaningful touch or touch a loved one with a special gift. And, most of all, I hope it encourages you to get those fingers in the mud and play. I know it did for me.

Tracy White

How to Use This Book

Whether you're a scrapbooker, photographer or crafter, or you simply want to explore your artistic side, this book will motivate you to create.

From meaningful scrapbook albums to personalized gifts and home decor, the following projects will serve as a constant source of inspiration. Whether you've got an hour or a day, a room full of supplies or just a few odds and ends, there's something here for you.

Although the projects are grouped into chapters, consider each idea on its own. For example, every book in the "album" chapter can become a gift when tailored to the recipient or serve as home decor when displayed for all to see. Follow the examples exactly, or change the style or color to suit your needs. You'll find that the creations in this book can fit any theme, match any decor or be the perfect gift for anyone on your list.

As you read the book and take in the sights, let them stimulate your imagination. Find an idea you love and make it your own. Preserve a memory, produce an heirloom or spruce up a room in your home. Above all, enjoy the process.

Scrapbook albums run the gamut of subjects and styles, encompassing everything from a baby's arrival to a memoir of a loved one from a past generation. Whatever the shape, size or level of complexity, the result is the same—a window of time preserved with irreplaceable photos and written details. Read on to discover how you can capture the events and milestones in yours or others' lives before the moments fade to memory.

Milestones **by Helen McCain**

Here's an "all about me" album that can grow as you do. By using a pail to collect and store finished scrapbook pages, Helen McCain designed a project she can work on whenever inspiration strikes or milestones occur.

How To:

Purchase a lunch-pail album and use the included inserts as background pages. Create mini scrapbook pages with photos, patterned paper and accents. To conserve space, write your journaling on index cards to slip behind the photos. Add to the album as you have new experiences or celebrate new accomplishments.

Helen's Tip:

When creating an autobiographical album, think about what you want to share with those who will view it. Start with a few highlights or current goals, then add new scrapbook pages as events occur.

EXTERIOR BOX
Supplies *Lunch box and letter stickers:* BasicGrey; *Patterned paper:* Scenic Route Paper Co.; *Transfer paper:* Lasertran Inkjet; *Printed twill and tags:* foof-a-La, Autumn Leaves; *Twill:* Bobbin Ribbon; *Shrink plastic:* Polyshrink; *Lace:* Making Memories; *Fastener:* K&Company; *Other:* Silk flowers and ribbon.

MILESTONES TITLE PAGE
Supplies *Patterned papers:* Scenic Route Paper Co.; *Tags:* BasicGrey; *Shrink plastic:* Polyshrink; *Index tab:* Making Memories; *Foam stamp:* Heidi Swapp for Advantus; *Paper flower:* Prima; *Computer font:* P22 Cezanne, downloaded from the Internet; *Other:* Ribbon.

MEMORIES
Supplies *Patterned papers:* BasicGrey, Scenic Route Paper Co. and Autumn Leaves; *Transparency:* K&Company; *Rickrack:* Heidi Swapp for Advantus; *Rub-on:* Scenic Route Paper Co.; *Quote:* KI Memories; *Leaves and flower:* Helen's own designs.

VEGEMITE
Supplies *Patterned paper:* BasicGrey; *Foam stamps:* Heidi Swapp for Advantus; *Ribbon:* American Crafts; *Acrylic paint:* Making Memories; *Paper flower:* Prima; *Rub-ons:* Autumn Leaves; *Transparency:* Grafix; *Computer font:* P22 Cezanne, downloaded from the Internet.

A child on a farm sees a plane fly by overhead and dreams of a faraway place – a traveler on the plane sees the farmhouse and dreams of home. –Carl Burns

Then one day you discover that Vegemite is now available in America...

And all is right in the world

Me. The Facts. by Candace Leonard

A scrapbook doesn't always need to include details about the past. Candace Leonard used mini file folders as the cover and pages for a slice-of-life album that provides quick glimpses at what's important to her at this point in time.

How To:

To create the album structure, bind six mini file folders by punching holes through the spines and binding with ribbon. Assign each folder a subject, then create mini scrapbook pages to support the theme with photos (resized to fit the small format), journaling and a variety of patterned papers and embellishments.

Candace's Tips:

Using file folders made the album easy to create because they gave me instant sections and filler pages. Look through your stash for different items to bind your album, like ribbon, brads or metal rings.

Supplies *Patterned papers:* KI Memories, Anna Griffin, BasicGrey and Autumn Leaves; *File folders:* Autumn Leaves; *Stickers:* KI Memories, 7gypsies and Scrapworks; *Rub-ons:* KI Memories and Autumn Leaves; *Buckle:* Li'l Davis Designs; *Acrylic accents and ribbon:* KI Memories; *Rubber stamps:* Postmodern Design and Catslife Press; *Stamping ink:* Memories, Stewart Superior Corporation; *Mini tags:* Making Memories; *Acrylic letters:* Heidi Swapp for Advantus; *Clear clip:* Artistic Expressions; *Computer font:* AL Worn Machine, downloaded from *www.twopeasinabucket.com.*

the **B**eth quiz

HOW WELL DO YOU KNOW ME

The Beth Quiz by Beth Opel

When designing a unique "all about me" book, let your personality shine. As a teacher, Beth Opel knew a quiz format was a natural choice for hers. She instantly engages the reader by asking questions and using interactive elements to reveal answers that provide facts about her life, personality and interests.

How To:

Purchase a pre-assembled, blank mini album, then create scrapbook pages with a question-and-answer format. Include interactive elements, such as pull-out journaling and questions (with answers in back) slipped into pockets or tucked behind flaps.

Beth's Tip:

Use the quiz format for a family or friendship album as well. For example, ask the reader to delineate the differences between siblings with questions like "Allison or Andrew?" Then create pages featuring their achievements, antics or quotes.

COVER
Supplies *Album:* Die Cuts With a View; *Textured cardstock:* Prism Papers; *Patterned papers:* Bo-Bunny Press and Urban Lily; *Stickers:* Pebbles Inc. (flowers), Autumn Leaves (epoxy circles); *Rub-on letters:* Making Memories; *Ribbon and rub-on flower:* KI Memories; *Paper flowers:* Making Memories (large yellow), Prima (small); *Metal album corners:* 7gypsies; *Eyelet brad:* Pebbles Inc.; *Brads:* Creative Impressions and Making Memories; *Dimensional-ink pen:* Liquid Appliqué, Marvy Uchida; *Computer fonts:* Hurricane, Triforce and Xerography, downloaded from the Internet; Arial and Script MT Bold, Microsoft Word.

AWKWARD OR ATHLETIC?
Supplies *Textured cardstock:* Prism Papers; *Patterned papers:* Urban Lily and Die Cuts With a View; *Stickers:* Bo-Bunny Press; *Ribbon:* SEI; *Rickrack:* EK Success; *Flower brad:* Creative Impressions; *Rub-ons:* KI Memories; *Dimensional-ink pen:* Liquid Appliqué, Marvy Uchida; *Computer fonts:* Arial, Microsoft Word; Cheapskate Fill and Weltron Urban, downloaded from the Internet.

ADVENTUROUS OR PLAY IT SAFE?
Supplies *Textured cardstock:* Prism Papers; *Patterned papers:* Anna Griffin, Close To My Heart and K&Company; *Felt pocket:* Kimberly Hodges, K&Company; *Dimensional sticker:* Marcella by Kay; *Paper flowers:* Prima; *Acrylic circle embellishments and rub-on flower:* KI Memories; *Silk flower:* Creating Keepsakes; *Corner rounder:* EK Success; *Brad:* Making Memories; *Dimensional-ink pen:* Liquid Appliqué, Marvy Uchida; *Computer fonts:* Arial, Microsoft Word; Tagettes Plus and An Creon, downloaded from the Internet.

Everyday Album **by Traci Turchin**

Life moves so quickly. Are there details you want to remember but know you'll forget? Traci Turchin found a solution with a pocket-filled project designed to retain and record tidbits of "ordinary" life that make her smile, such as notes, mementos, humorous quotes and more.

How To:

Purchase an album and fill it with interesting bits and pieces. Create calendar pages with photos on some of the dates, then add clippings, receipts or notes. You can attach library pockets or envelopes to the pages using double-stick tape to fill with mementos of your day-to-day life.

Traci's Tip:

Don't worry about making this album too orderly. Throw in newspaper clippings and notes in a collage-like manner, then write about what they mean to you.

Supplies *Software:* Adobe Photoshop CS, Adobe Systems; *Album:* 7gypsies; *Patterned papers:* KI Memories, BasicGrey, Autumn Leaves and Chatterbox; *Letter stickers:* American Crafts; *Letter stamps:* A Muse Artstamps; *Pen:* Pigment Pro, American Crafts; *Computer font:* Universe, downloaded from *www.linotype.com.*

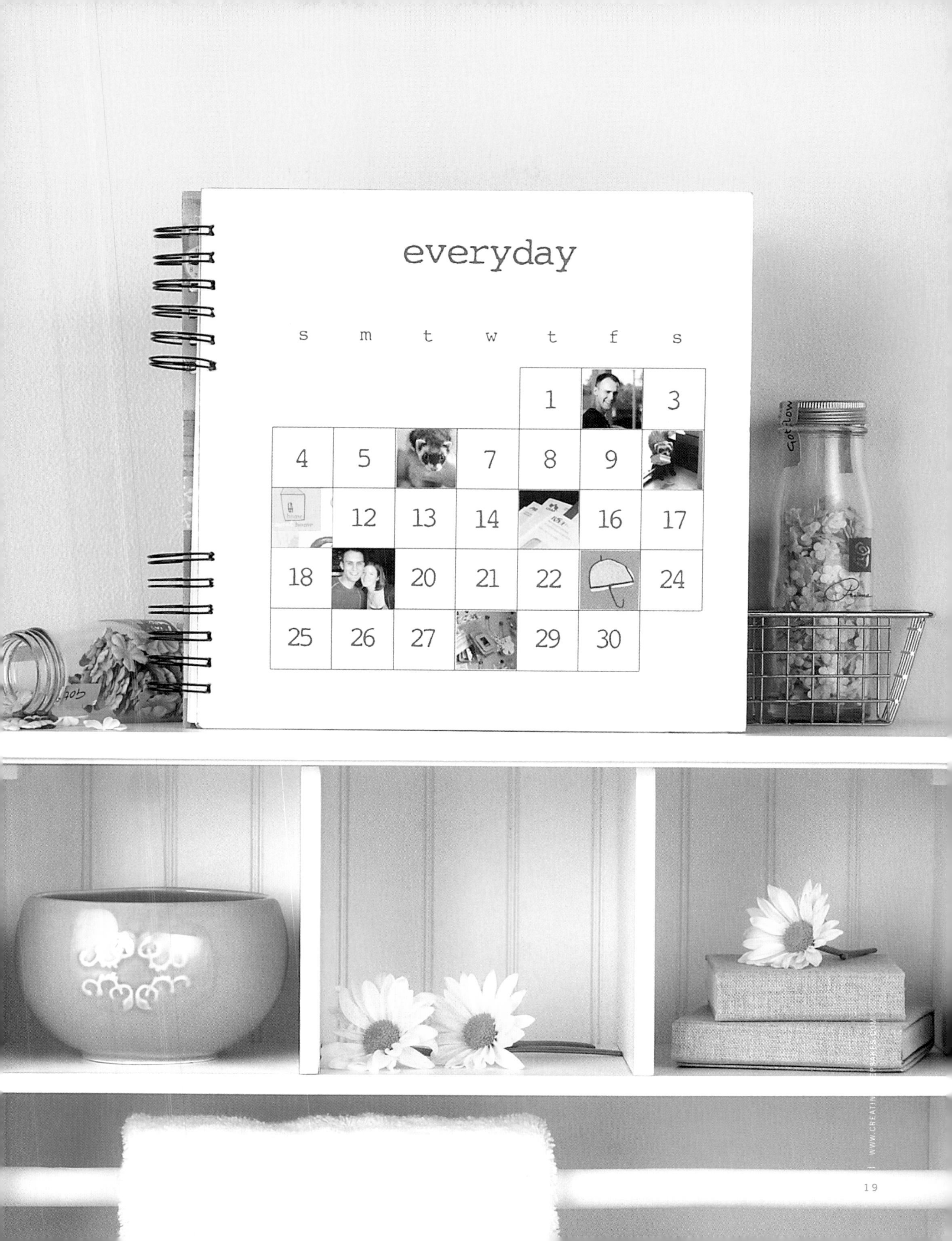
everyday
s m t w t f s
1 3
4 5 7 8 9
12 13 14 16 17
18 20 21 22 24
25 26 27 29 30

FAMILY
ALBUM

Who We Are **by Vanessa Reyes**

Vanessa Reyes loves displaying her family's photos and memories throughout her home, and a creative chipboard album was the perfect project for an entryway shelf. With a page dedicated to each member of the family, the scrapbook provides a quick glimpse of everyone's interests, characteristics and personalities.

How To:

Cut chipboard to size and cover with patterned paper. Add a photo, accents and journaling (printed on vellum) to each piece of chipboard. Punch holes through the pages and use a beaded chain to connect them.

Vanessa's Tip:

If you're designing a gift album for someone, but you're running short on time, try creating a mini book. It's just as meaningful as a large scrapbook—and much quicker to complete.

Supplies *Patterned papers:* American Crafts; *Letter stickers:* American Crafts, Heidi Grace Designs and Mrs. Grossman's; *Chipboard letters:* Heidi Swapp for Advantus; *Rub-ons:* KI Memories; *Decorative tags:* Pebbles Inc.; *Shaker-box stickers:* Christina Cole for Provo Craft; *"Boo" plate, mini brads, metal word and foam stamps:* Making Memories; *Sticker strip:* 7gypsies; *Photo corner:* Chatterbox; *Woven label:* me & my BIG ideas; *Ribbon:* May Arts, Li'l Davis Designs and Making Memories; *Other:* Chipboard, beaded chain, slide holder and vellum.

A Story About Us by Allison Kimball

Do your children love to hear stories about their lives or how your family came to be? Try creating an album that provides a cute, casual family history like the one designed by Allison Kimball. Allison created the durable project over an old board book because she knew her children would look at it over and over again.

How To:

Create the title on your computer and print it on photo paper. Decoupage patterned paper, stickers and your title onto the cover of a board book. Create each page by adding photos and journaling, then coating with decoupage medium for durability.

Allison's Tip:

The story-album format is a great way to share the story of your birth, school days or any event in your life.

Supplies *Patterned papers:* Autumn Leaves, Making Memories, KI Memories, Daisy D's Paper Co. and 7gypsies; *Rub-ons:* Autumn Leaves, K&Company, Chatterbox, Doodlebug Design, Li'l Davis Designs and Melissa Frances; *Mask and chipboard numbers and letters:* Heidi Swapp for Advantus; *Letter stickers:* Making Memories, Doodlebug Design and American Crafts; *Fabric flowers and tags:* Autumn Leaves; *Gems and pearls:* Making Memories; *Brads:* American Crafts; *Computer fonts:* MA Sexy and Century Gothic, downloaded from the Internet; *Other:* Board book.

The Games We Play by Sande Krieger

An actual game board and pieces form the inventive cover for an album Sande Krieger created to document her family's love of board games. Individual scrapbook pages preserve memories of the "whens, wheres and whys."

How To:

Design the album by removing the pages from an old hardback book, then attaching game boards to the front and back covers with strong liquid adhesive. Adorn the cover with game pieces. Trim and stitch page protectors to fit inside the book and secure them with ribbon tied through holes in the book's binding.

Sande's Tips:

It's so important to write the memories down, so I like to focus on the journaling first. Keep the album simple by coming up with two or three layout designs and repeating them with different patterned papers or colors.

BOOK COVER & INSIDE COVER
Supplies *Patterned papers:* Scenic Route Paper Co.; *Chipboard letter:* Li'l Davis Designs; *Gaffer tape:* 7gypsies; *Woven letter, jump rings and letter tiles:* Making Memories; *Letter stickers:* EK Success; *Chipboard tag:* Daisy D's Paper Co.; *Waxed floss:* Scrapworks; *Ribbon:* May Arts; *Other:* Sorry game board; assorted game pieces from Monopoly, Sorry, Life, Pick Two and Clue; poker chips.

TABLE OF CONTENTS
Supplies *Patterned papers:* KI Memories; *Computer fonts:* 2Peas Cowgirl, 2Peas Quick Wit, 2Peas Gift and 2Peas Tokyo Girl, downloaded from *www.twopeasinabucket.com.*

CHESS
Supplies *Patterned papers:* KI Memories; *Bookplate and tag:* Making Memories; *Acrylic paint:* Golden; *Epoxy embellishments:* Provo Craft; *Clock hands:* Walnut Hollow; *Letter stickers:* SEI and Scenic Route Paper Co.; *Label tape:* Dymo; *Brads:* Creative Impressions; *Computer fonts:* AL Eyewitness and AL Outloud, downloaded from *www.twopeasinabucket.com;* Agency FB and Bernhardt MT Condensed, downloaded from the Internet.

SORRY
Supplies *Patterned papers:* SEI; *Chipboard letter and safety pins:* Li'l Davis Designs; *Circle and long red-and-blue polka-dot embellishment:* Christina Cole for Provo Craft; *Tags:* Making Memories; *Ribbon:* May Arts and Making Memories; *Letter stamps:* Postmodern Design and Hero Arts; *Stamping ink:* Ranger Industries.

Values Are Our Foundation by Traci Turchin

Every family is built on a foundation of values and traditions. Traci Turchin pays tribute to them with an album that outlines the values passed down through her family, and why they're held so dear.

How To:

Cover the album with patterned paper and add accents and a title. Use photo-editing software to create background pages on white cardstock. Create photo collages and adhere them to the background pages.

Traci's Tips:

This album is simple enough that it could also make a quick gift album dedicated to any theme. Although I created these scrapbook pages using my digital software, you can also hand-make them.

Supplies *Software:* Adobe Photoshop CS, Adobe Systems; *Album:* 7gypsies; *Patterned papers:* KI Memories; *Rubber stamps:* A Muse Artstamps; *Computer font:* Universe, downloaded from *www.linotype.com*.

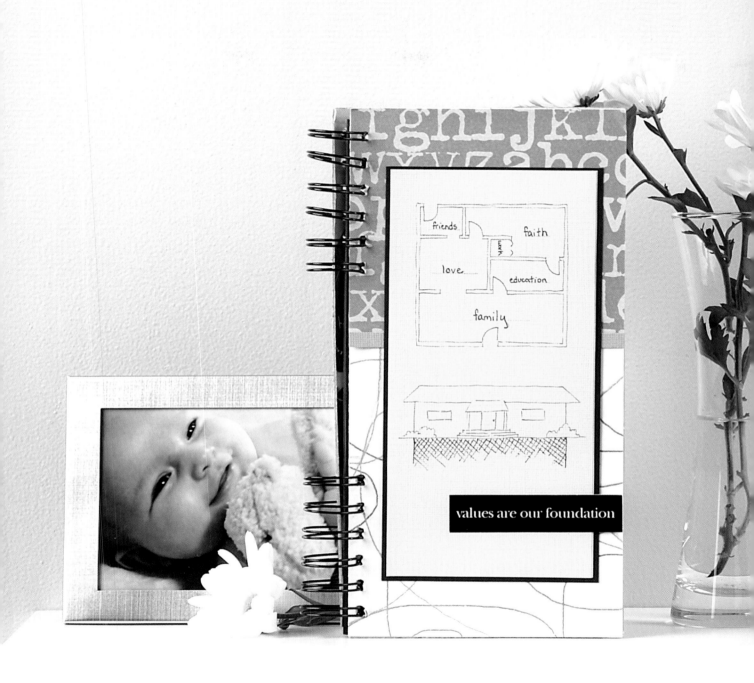

friends
faith
work
love
education
family

values are our foundation

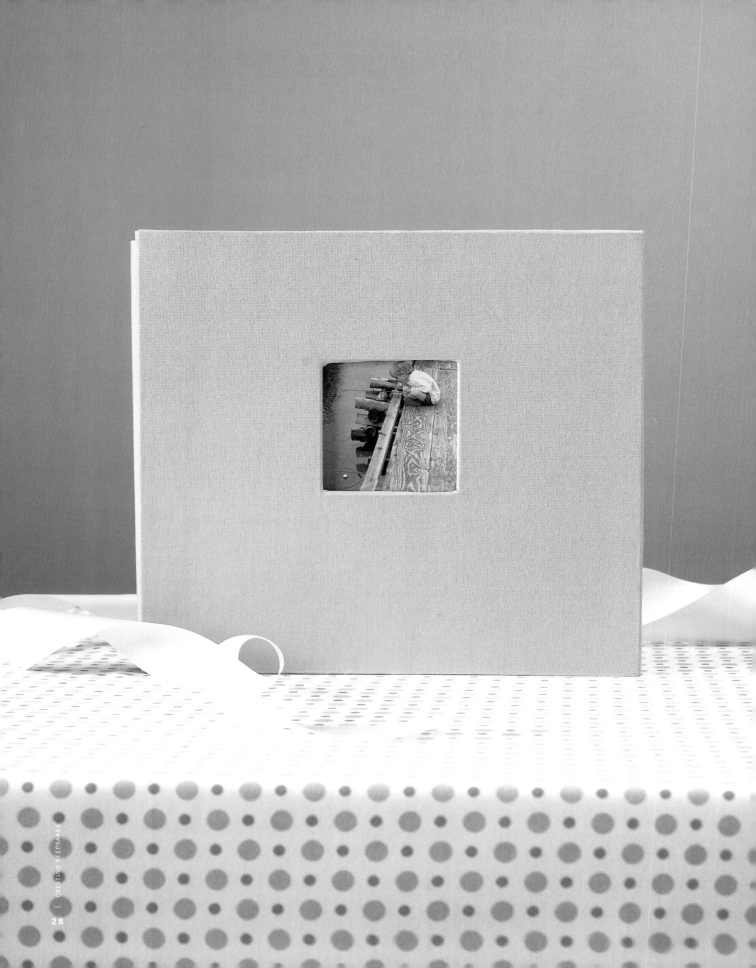

Bat Mitzvah of Taylor Rachel by Allison Landy

Albums dedicated to a single event are an ideal way to commemorate the celebration. Allison Landy wanted her daughter to remember her Bat Mitzvah—the hard work, the fun and the importance of the ceremony. The use of Jewish liturgy as journaling and elements from the event add meaning to the album.

How To:

Sort photos to determine which will fit into each "chapter" of the album. Sketch the layout designs. Cut cardstock and patterned paper to size, then embellish the scrapbook pages with rubber stamps, ribbon and chipboard pieces.

Allison's Tip:

Pre-planning is the most important timesaver when creating an event album. Sorting photos ahead of time and determining what parts of the event to highlight make the process much easier.

BAT MITZVAH OF TAYLOR RACHEL
Supplies *Patterned paper, border stickers and photo corners:* Scrapworks; *Rubber stamp:* Stampin' Up!; *Letter stamps:* Make Believe and Technique Tuesday; *Stamping ink:* StazOn, Tsukineko; *Rub-on:* Sonnets. Creative Imaginations; *Paper flowers:* Making Memories (white) and Prima (brown); *Charm:* Annalis Scraptique; *Punch:* EK Success; *Pearl pin:* Boxer Scrapbook Productions; *Ribbon:* American Crafts; *Buckle:* Nunn Designs; *Chipboard circle:* Technique Tuesday; *Brads:* Lost Art Treasures; *Pen:* Pigment Pro, American Crafts; *Rhinestone brad:* Magic Scraps.

Graduation **by Joy Uzarraga**

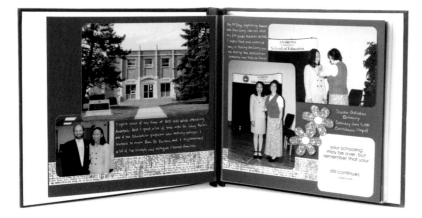

Show your school spirit by designing an album with your school's colors. Joy Uzarraga re-created her graduation album (once just filled with photos and stickers) to make it even more meaningful. This time around, she added journaling, graduation-themed quotes and rubber-stamped images.

How To:

Print quotes on white cardstock and trim. Embellish the front cover with ribbon and insert a quote. To create each layout, add a word border, quote, photos, journaling and rubber-stamped designs.

Joy's Tip:

It's easy to go "camera happy" during events like birthday parties and graduations. Don't feel pressure to include every single photo in your scrapbook; choose only the best or most important photos.

Supplies *Textured cardstock:* Die Cuts With a View; *Patterned paper:* Art Warehouse, Creative Imaginations; *Rubber stamps:* Creative Imaginations and Limited Edition Rubberstamps; *Stamping ink:* ColorBox Fluid Chalk, Clearsnap; *Slide mounts:* Narratives, Creative Imaginations; *Ribbon:* C.M. Offray & Son; *Pen:* Gelly Roll, Sakura; *Computer fonts:* Century Gothic, downloaded from the Internet; P22 Cezanne, downloaded from *www.typefoundry.com.*

graduation
is not the end;
it's the beginning.
-orrin hatch

Forever and Always *by Jennifer Gallacher*

In addition to larger albums commemorating your wedding, create a separate mini book as a bonus keepsake. Simple embellishments and page designs, as well as the small size, make Jennifer Gallacher's project a quick, portable way to showcase cherished images.

How To:

Cover a white 6" x 6" album with ribbon and embellishments. Add photos, patterned paper and embellishments to white background pages. Instead of journaling, use wedding stickers or rub-on phrases to help unify the album.

Jennifer's Tip:

When creating a mini album, save time by pre-cutting all papers to size. For my album, for example, I trimmed all the paper to 6" x 6" before putting the pages together.

COVER
Supplies *Album:* Making Memories; *Patterned paper and rub-on phrase:* Déjà Views, The C-Thru Ruler Co.; *Ribbon:* C.M. Offray & Son and Creative Imaginations; *Pearl buckles and plaque:* Li'l Davis Designs; *Charm:* Karen Foster Design; *Jump ring, bookplate and brads:* Making Memories.

LOVE OF MY LIFE
Supplies *Patterned paper:* K&Company; *Metal frame, jump ring, buttons and embroidery floss:* Making Memories; *Mini brads:* Junkitz (blue) and Colorbök; *Label:* Autumn Leaves; *Stamping ink:* Memories, Stewart Superior Corporation; *Date stamp:* Staples; *Ribbon:* Li'l Davis Designs; *Rub-on phrase:* Déjà Views, The C-Thru Ruler Co.; *Charm:* Karen Foster Design.

FOREVER AND ALWAYS
Supplies *Patterned papers:* K&Company and The C-Thru Ruler Co.; *Ribbon:* Creative Imaginations; *Cork and charm:* Karen Foster Design; *Jump ring:* Making Memories; *Flower:* Li'l Davis Designs; *Rub-on phrase:* Déjà Views, The C-Thru Ruler Co.

TO HAVE AND TO HOLD
Supplies *Patterned papers:* K&Company and The C-Thru Ruler Co.; *Cork:* Karen Foster Design; *Letter stickers, tan ribbon and buckle:* Li'l Davis Designs; *Pink ribbon:* Creative Imaginations; *Rub-on phrase:* Déjà Views, The C-Thru Ruler Co.

HOPE

faith hope love

Wedding

Journey to Motherhood by Amber Ries

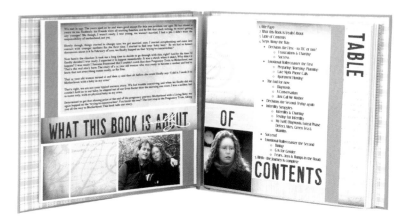

Amber Ries wanted an album to chronicle what it took for her to become a mother— a journey filled with hope, loss, struggle, fear and finally the joy of giving birth to a healthy baby girl. She hopes that one day her daughter will treasure the story of how she came to be.

How To:

Sketch and plan the album. Select papers and photos, then create "framework" pages to separate each "chapter." Place coordinating filler pages in each chapter.

Amber's Tip:

Decide beforehand what stories you want to tell. Create an outline that will become the table of contents for the scrapbook; it will help you remember what you want to include in the book.

Supplies *Patterned paper:* BasicGrey; *Rub-ons:* KI Memories; *Paper flowers:* Prima; *Computer fonts:* 18th Century and Dearest Swash, downloaded from the Internet; AL Highlight, downloaded from *www.twopeasinabucket.com.*

M IS FOR *motherhood*

bloom & grow

h

Bloom & Grow **by Joanna Bolick**

Do you have a lot of photos but not a lot of time? When Joanna Bolick became overwhelmed with the number of images she had of her second child, she decided to make a simple album to show off the ones she loved most. By using photos that focus on the baby's personality rather than facts and figures, Joanna's project captures the everyday moments that fly by all too quickly.

How To:

Apply rub-ons to the cover and the inside of the front and back covers. Create each layout with a large photo, a single-word title and handwritten journaling. Embellish the pages sparsely with ribbon, paper and stickers.

Joanna's Tip:

The key to a quick-and-easy album? Keep it simple. Use large photos, pick a few complementary papers and get to work!

Supplies *Album:* Making Memories; *Patterned papers:* Urban Lily, Fontwerks, Chatterbox, Sandylion, Autumn Leaves and Provo Craft; *Textured cardstock:* Bazzill Basics Paper; *Letter stickers:* Scrapworks and Heidi Swapp for Advantus; *Rub-ons:* Scrapworks (flowers), Making Memories (letters) and Autumn Leaves (stitching); *Ribbon:* Scrapworks; *Fabric flower sticker:* foof-a-La, Autumn Leaves; *Photo corners:* Heidi Swapp for Advantus.

Luke from Day One by Melissa Chapman

Here's Melissa Chapman's ultimate "brag book"—an album that features precious photos and facts from her son's first year. As her son grows, Melissa continues to expand the album and plans to give it to her parents as a comprehensive record of their grandson's memories and milestones.

How To:

Cover two pieces of mat board with corrugated cardstock. Embellish the cover with letters mounted on chipboard. Attach page protectors between the covers with oversized brads. Create 6" x 6" pages using a coordinating line of products.

Melissa's Tip:

If you're going to create your album later, set your favorite photos from each month aside and keep a journal with lists of events or observations for each day so you don't forget.

Supplies *Patterned papers:* KI Memories; *Textured cardstock:* Bazzill Basics Paper and The Paper Company; *Brads:* Creative Impressions; *Woven label tab:* Scrapworks; *Computer fonts:* GeosansLight and P22 Corinthia, downloaded from the Internet.

| WWW.CREATINGKEEPSAKES.COM

Boys Will Be Boys by Mary Larson

If you're the mother of sons, as Mary Larson is, you undoubtedly have stacks of these "boys will be boys" photos—shots of them being mischievous, silly or adventurous. A compact disc case provides an inventive format to keep several photos together, and its shape gives the album a whimsical feel.

How To:
Inside the CD case, cut the top and bottom off the CD protectors, leaving 1" strips attached to the spine. Cut black cardstock circles to fit inside the case, two for each page. Attach the circles (which become the background pages) to the strips, one on each side (attaching them to the spine and hiding the strips at the same time). Add photos and embellishments to the pages and album cover.

Mary's Tip:
To simplify the album, find a square CD case, which will eliminate the need to cut circular pages. Or use a circle-shaped case, but simply stack the circular scrapbook pages inside.

Supplies *Patterned papers:* Arctic Frog; *Rubber stamps:* Scrappy Cat; *Brads:* American Crafts; *Ribbon and rickrack:* Michaels; *CD case:* Target.

The Art of Grandma Eva by Carey Johnson

Who says heritage albums have to be subdued? Carey Johnson created a rich, colorful album to pay tribute to her grandmother's talents, such as cooking, painting and sewing. Featuring poignant photos and the sweet memories that surround them, Carey's project will surely be cherished for generations to come.

How To:

Select a combination of colorful patterned papers and die-cut shapes that evoke an "old-fashioned" feeling. Choose heritage photos and write journaling that reflects what you know and feel about them.

Carey's Tip:

Start any heritage project by sorting through the stories you already know. Brainstorm what you recall about the topic and find photos that represent those memories.

Supplies *Patterned papers:* Autumn Leaves; *Rubber stamp:* Paper Inspirations; *Stamping ink:* StazOn, Tsukineko; *Metal letters:* American Crafts; *Rub-ons:* K&Company; *Big button, big brads and washers:* Bazzill Basics Paper; *Corner rounder, silver stick-ons and flower punch:* EK Success; *Circle punch:* Marvy Uchida; *Large flower:* Chic; *Computer fonts:* Benguait BK BT, Century Gothic, Adler and 60's, downloaded from the Internet; 2Peas Frappachino, downloaded from *www.twopeasinabucket.com*; Arial, Microsoft Word; *Other:* Ribbon and jute.

And moreover, to succeed, the artist must
possess the courageous soul...the brave soul.
The soul that dares and defies.
--Kate Chopin

eva

ART

WWW.CREATINGKEEPSAKES.COM

Catherine by Jenni Bowlin

If you've ever wanted to learn more about a relative's life, here's the perfect idea: Jenni Bowlin gave her grandmother a simple journal filled with questions. When it was returned, Jenni combined the answers with photos to create a beautiful look at her grandmother's childhood and beyond.

How To:

Assemble notes for the project based on questions you've asked a loved one to answer. Use the answers to create journaling around the photos. Embellish the pages with rubber-stamped images, stickers and flowers. Add photos to the cover and embellish with ribbon and a vintage-looking pin.

Jenni's Tip:

Even if you don't keep traditional scrapbooks, this is a small-scale project you can create to commemorate a loved one's life. The journal style makes it easy to write and organize.

Supplies *Album and label stickers:* Making Memories; *Paper flowers:* Prima; *Rubber stamps:* Stampotique Originals and Stampin' Up!; *Other:* Ribbon, vintage rhinestones and rhinestone pin.

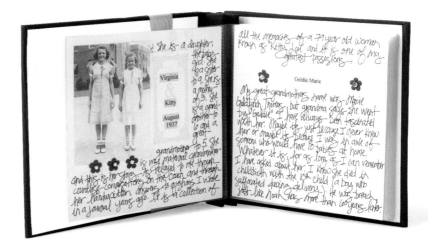

Circle Journals

by Rachel Thomae

A circle journal is a book that is circulated among friends or family members. Each person fills in one page of the book and then sends it along to the next person. This is a wonderful way to share favorite family memories, to learn more about your friends (and yourself!) and to explore your creativity.

There are endless circle journal variations. For example, you might want to start a family recipe journal, where you ask each member to record her favorite family recipe and share a photograph of the completed dish. When the journals are finished, each participant will have her own handmade family cookbook.

Another idea? Use a circle journal to share pictures of your children with their grandparents. Start with two blank books so you'll both have a copy to keep at the end of the year. Every month, add a new picture of your children; ask the grandparents to write their thoughts about the picture and send it back to you. At the end of the year, you'll have a treasured keepsake that documents your children's growth and development.

Want to start your own circle journal project? Follow these four steps:

❶ Gather a group of friends or family members who want to participate in your circle journal activity.

❷ Decide on a theme for your circle journal. For example, consider creating a circle journal on the topic of friendship or favorite family stories.

❸ Have each person in the group purchase or make a blank journal. It's often best if the journals are all the same size and shape so that you'll be creating the same size page in each book that comes your way.

❹ Decide on a time frame for the journals to be completed and give everyone a copy of your journal schedule. Ask members to check in via e-mail when they receive and mail out the circle journal.

Christmas 2005 by Sande Krieger

The holidays are often the busiest time of the year. But they're also some of the most memory-filled times. Make sure you keep your camera handy and snap photos of all those special moments. When you have a few minutes, choose the best photos and create scrapbook pages that highlight your memories. Looking back at the holiday memories is sure to become a favorite yearly tradition.

How To:

Choose 2–3 photos from each of the events you snapped photos of. (Don't feel like you have to use all of the photos.) Then, design pages highlighting the best memories and details of the holiday season. Use patterned papers and other themed accents to create an album filled with warm memories of the holidays. Finally, design a cover that highlights the year and theme of the album

Sande's Tips:

Choose an album that is easy to add pages to. This three-ring album allows me to easily slip in pages as I create them. And be sure to capture the personality of your family by capturing those quirky expressions and inside jokes.

Supplies *Album:* Scrapworks; *Patterned papers:* AJSmith's Birdie for *www.digichick.com*, Carolee's Creations, KI Memories and Scenic Route Paper Co.; *Rub-ons:* Scrapworks, Autumn Leaves, Scenic Route Paper Co., EK Success and Heidi Swapp for Advantus; *Letter stamps:* Hero Arts and Just Rite; *Stamping ink:* Fluid Chalk, Clearsnap; *Epoxy numbers:* Art Warehouse, Creative Imaginations; *Photo turn:* 7gypsies; *Ribbon:* American Crafts; *Brad:* Making Memories; *Digital brushes:* MaryAnn Wise; Rhonna Farrer, downloaded from *www.twopeasinabucket.com*; *Computer fonts:* 2Peas Happy Go Lucky, 2Peas Journaling Dinbats, 2Peas Essential and AL Landscape, downloaded from *www.twopeasinabucket.com*; Century, Microsoft Word; Purple Boxers, downloaded from *www.abstractfonts.com*; Misproject, downloaded from *www.misprintedtype.com*.

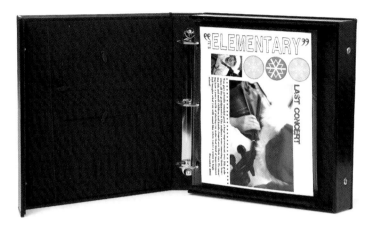

WWW.CREATINGKEEPSAKES.COM

24 Hours in NYC by Allison Landy

After a one-day, whirlwind trip to New York City, Allison Landy wanted an album to remind her of the adventure. A mini book was the perfect size to showcase enough photos to impart a sense of the excursion.

How To:

Create the cover by coating two chipboard squares with acrylic paint. Accordion-fold two pieces of cardstock and adhere them to the inside of each cover. Add photos and embellishments to the cardstock.

Allison's Tip:

When creating a mini album, "wallet size" photos (approximately 2" x 3") are the perfect size to fit without cropping.

Supplies *Textured cardstock:* Prism Papers; *Chipboard:* Bazzill Basics Paper; *Chipboard shape:* Making Memories; *Epoxy letters:* Karen Foster Design; *Bottle-cap sticker:* Design Originals; *Brad:* The Happy Hammer; *Rub-ons:* My Mind's Eye; *Letter stamps:* Ma Vinci's Reliquary; *Stamping ink:* Distress Ink, Ranger Industries; StazOn, Tsukineko; *Acrylic paint:* Krylon and Plaid Enterprises; *Pen:* Pigment Pro, American Crafts; *Computer font:* Adler, downloaded from the Internet; *Other:* Date stamp and folder clip.

Tahitian Honeymoon **by Joy Uzarraga**

Are the photos from your honeymoon sitting in a box or in sleeve-type photo albums? After realizing that she and her husband were beginning to forget some of the details of their trip, Joy Uzarraga decided to create a mini album that includes memorable images and their handwritten recollections.

How To:

Cover the front and back album covers with patterned paper. Add photos to the pages on the right, and embellish the left side with stickers and decorative tape. Handwrite your journaling.

Joy's Tip:

For straight handwritten journaling, draw lines lightly with a pencil and ruler. Write your journaling in pencil, trace over it with a pen, then erase the pencil lines.

Supplies *Album:* Li'l Davis Designs; *Patterned paper:* Rusty Pickle; *Decorative tape:* Heidi Swapp for Advantus; *Palm trees:* Jolee's By You, Sticko for EK Success; *Chipboard heart:* Making Memories; *Letter stamps:* Hero Arts; *Pen:* Zig Writer, EK Success; *Stamping ink:* StazOn, Tsukineko.

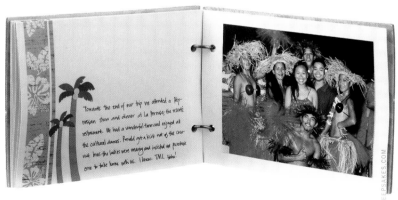

Summer 2005 Road Trip by Laurie Stamas

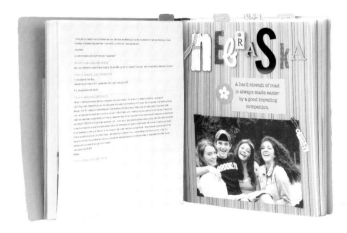

Do you keep a diary as you travel? When Laurie Stamas and her daughters traveled 6,000 miles across the country, they posted adventures and photos to their "blog" (a web log on the Internet). These entries became the perfect journaling for a travel album, complete with a DVD of their escapades.

How To:

Print out blog or diary entries. Design your title pages with photos to introduce each album chapter. Create pages featuring pictures, journaling, memorabilia and embellishments. Burn a CD or DVD of vacation photos and music to include in the album.

Laurie's Tip:

Blog entries make the perfect journaling for scrapbook pages. Copy and paste them into a word-processing program—that way you can size each entry to fit your layout.

Supplies *Album and buttons:* SEI; *Patterned papers:* KI Memories and Carolee's Creations; *Tags, ribbon, acrylic frame and quotes:* KI Memories; *License plate:* Sticker Studio; *Elastic:* 7gypsies; *Acrylic paint, chipboard letters, tags, paper flowers, pins, brads, washers and jump rings:* Making Memories; *Rub-ons:* Autumn Leaves and Scrapworks; *Chipboard shape and iron-on letters:* Heidi Swapp for Advantus; *Fabric quotes and words:* me & my BIG ideas; *Large "I" monogram:* My Mind's Eye; *Charms:* The Card Connection; *Stamping ink:* Ranger Industries; *Fabric letters:* Scrapworks; *Sponge stamps and chipboard letter:* Li'l Davis Designs; *Photo corners:* Canson; *Other:* Route 66 decal and large iron-on numbers.

ROAD TRIP

travel

journey

Summer 2005

ROUTE 66

Drive Through **by Annie Weis**

As you drive through a picturesque city, take the time to capture some scenic shots from the road. Annie Weis included her glimpses of San Francisco in a stylish mini album with a design that spotlights her incredible photos.

How To:

Purchase an album that can be disassembled. Print the photo captions directly onto the pages. Add photos to the right-hand pages above the captions and embellish both sides with patterned paper, rub-ons, epoxy stickers and photo corners.

Annie's Tip:

For an album that keeps the focus on your photos, mimic the look of a photography or coffee table book and use simple captions instead of lengthy journaling.

Supplies *Patterned papers:* Angela Adams Stationery, Chronicle Books; *Letter stickers and monograms:* American Crafts; *Ribbon:* May Arts; *Epoxy stickers:* Autumn Leaves and Provo Craft; *Bumper sticker:* Scrapworks; *Photo corners:* Heidi Swapp for Advantus; *Pen:* Sharpie, Sanford; *Computer font:* Georgia, downloaded from the Internet.

Hawaii by Christy Tomlinson

After 10 years of marriage and five children, Christy Tomlinson and her husband took their first "real" vacation alone. Their time in Hawaii was such a bonding experience, she designed an album—filled with photos and detailed journaling about their adventures—as a reminder of how much the trip meant to her.

How To:

Disassemble a spiral chipboard album. Trim pages to size and add photos and embellishments. For the right-side pages, stamp images on white cardstock, then, once dry, print journaling over the designs. For the left-side pages, paint directly on the chipboard background pages and print journaling on transparencies as overlays. Decorate the album cover and reassemble the album.

Christy's Tips:

Save time by purchasing a preprinted mini album. Simplify the embellishments by using stickers instead of rubber stamps, and use handwritten journaling rather than computer printing.

Supplies *Chipboard album:* 7gypsies; *Patterned papers:* Chatterbox, American Crafts, Scapworks, NRN Designs, College Press and My Mind's Eye; *Ribbon:* Chatterbox, Making Memories, May Arts, All My Memories and American Crafts; *Rub-ons:* Chatterbox and Making Memories; *Foam stamps:* Heidi Swapp for Advantus; *Tag and bookplate:* Making Memories; *Flowers:* Prima and Li'l Davis Designs; *Computer font:* CK Chemistry, "Fresh Fonts" CD, *Creating Keepsakes.*

Paris by Sande Krieger

An extra-special trip requires an extra-special place to record all of the memories. Sande Krieger designed an elegant journal with photos, journaling tags and memorabilia that chronicles her family's journey to Paris. Gorgeous craftsmanship and an embossed metal cover give the project instant heirloom quality.

How To:

Remove the pages from an old book and cover the front and back with patterned paper. Dry-emboss copper squares and coat them with black paint. Use a towel to remove most of the paint and allow to dry. Move the flame from a long-handled lighter over the copper to change its color. Attach the copper to the book cover with liquid adhesive.

Sande's Tip:

A composition book can make a great travel record. I made a quick-and-easy Paris journal for a friend and attached pockets and envelopes for memorabilia.

COVER
Supplies *Copper metal:* Amaco; *Metal embossing tools:* Ten Seconds Studio; *Acrylic paint:* Making Memories; *Gaffer tape and patterned paper:* 7gypsies; *"Paris" label:* Cavallini & Co.; *Fabric for binding:* Jo-Ann Crafts; *Twill:* Scenic Route Paper Co.; *Ribbon:* May Arts; *Other:* Old book.

EIFFEL TOWER
Supplies *Patterned papers:* 7gypsies and Autumn Leaves; *Rub-ons:* Scenic Route Paper Co.; *Brads, "Landmark" tag and jump rings:* Making Memories; *Epoxy Eiffel Tower and patterned paper:* Creative Imaginations; *Specimen card:* 7gypsies; *"Moments" rubber stamps:* Just Rite; *Eiffel Tower, and page tab and tag die cuts:* Provo Craft; *Ribbon:* May Arts; *Bottle cap:* Design Originals; *Star:* Scrapworks; *"Joy" charm:* Nunn Design; *Key charm:* Frost Creek Charms; *Other:* Sun charm.

OBSERVATIONS AND 1, 2, 3 TAGS
Supplies *Patterned papers:* 7gypsies, Li'l Davis Designs and Daisy D's Paper Co.; *"Observations" tab:* 7gypsies; *Metal flowers, charm and flower strip:* Nunn Design; *Buttons:* 7gypsies; *Tag, jump rings and metal charm:* Making Memories; *Rickrack and ribbon:* May Arts; *Chipboard letters:* Li'l Davis Designs; *Paper clip:* EK Success; *Epoxy Eiffel Tower:* Provo Craft; *Letter stamps:* PSX Design, Postmodern Design, Hero Arts, Fontwerks, Just Rite and EK Success; *Stamping ink:* Clearsnap and Ranger Industries; *Rub-on number, letter and epoxy number:* Art Warehouse, Creative Imaginations; *"2" sticker:* Sticker Studio; *Epoxy "S":* Karen Foster Design; *Brads:* Creative Impressions.

WWW.CREATINGKEEPSAKES.COM

Our Vacation **by Heather Preckel**

A small album can be a great coffee table discussion piece and an eye-catching way to showcase some of your most interesting vacation photos and memories. Using a compact disc holder, Heather Preckel designed a piece that's also portable enough to show off at family functions.

How To:

Cut cardstock circles the size of CD sleeves. Add photos and embellish with different mediums, ribbon, brads and rub-ons. Adhere each mini layout to the CD sleeves. Decorate the cover.

Heather's Tip:

Have fun whenever you create a mini album like this! You can also use the CD sleeves as pockets for photos, journaling or other items.

Supplies *Textured cardstock:* Bazzill Basics Paper; *Patterned paper:* A2Z Essentials; *Ribbon:* May Arts, Michaels and C.M. Offray & Son; *Staples and CD case:* Target; *Brads and photo turns:* Junkitz; *Pen:* Uni-ball, Sanford; *Rub-ons:* Making Memories; *Double-sided tape and foam squares:* Therm O Web.

WWW.CREATINGKEEPSAKES.COM

Friendship **by Beth Wakulsky**

Have some of your best friendships been those you've shared with your pets? Beth Wakulsky designed a cheerful album to remind her children of the special bonds they've shared with the family pets, past and present. Beth's color scheme and album format can easily be adapted to honor friendships among people too!

How To:

Purchase coordinating papers, embellishments and an album. Create an introduction page and table of contents. Design the scrapbook pages to fit each category outlined on the table of contents page. Decorate the cover to fit the theme of the album.

Beth's Tip:

Select a color scheme ahead of time and don't purchase too many different products. It's much easier to create when you don't have so much to choose from! Using the same products throughout the album also gives it a sense of unity.

Supplies *Patterned papers:* Gin-X, Imagination Project; *Die Cuts With a View;* Provo Craft; *Ribbon:* Making Memories; Gin-X, Imagination Project; Queen & Co.; KI Memories; *Rub-ons:* KI Memories and Gin-X, Imagination Project; *Acrylic letters:* Heidi Swapp for Advantus; *Metal letters:* American Crafts; *Button letters:* Junkitz; *Letter tiles:* Doodlebug Design; *Cardboard letters, acrylic paint and staples:* Making Memories; *Stickers:* Making Memories and EK Success; *Tags:* Provo Craft, Junkitz and Making Memories; *Letter stamps:* Making Memories and PSX Design; *Stamping ink:* Vivid!, Clearsnap; VersaMagic, Tsukineko; *Brads:* Provo Craft and Making Memories; *Metal clips:* Jo-Ann Scrap Essentials; *Computer fonts:* Times New Roman, Microsoft Word; Linenstroke, "PrintMaster" CD, Broderbund; CK Sketch and CK Jot, "The Art of Creative Lettering" CD, *Creating Keepsakes.*

Our Pets by Michaela Young-Mitchell

Pay tribute to your pets' personalities with an album featuring photos and journaling that illustrate their best qualities. Michaela Young-Mitchell used a basic color scheme and similar shapes and elements throughout the project, which showcases the pets her children have loved and grown up with.

How To:

Create an album cover with chipboard, cardstock and ribbon. Tie the pages into the album and add photos, journaling and embellishments.

Michaela's Tip:

Save time by using a premade album. All you'll have to do is add photos, journaling and a few accents.

Supplies *Textured cardstock:* Prism Papers and Bazzill Basics Paper; *Rub-on letters and mailbox letters:* Making Memories; *Resin, gel stickers, brads, mini brads, brad bars and pet-tag sticker:* Karen Foster Design; *Die-cut letters:* QuicKutz; *Letter buttons:* Doodlebug Design; *Heart brad:* Provo Craft; *Flower:* Once Upon a Scribble; *Rickrack:* Wrights; *Ribbon:* Maya Road and C.M. Offray & Son; *Metal-rimmed tag:* Avery; *Pen:* Pigment Pro, American Crafts.

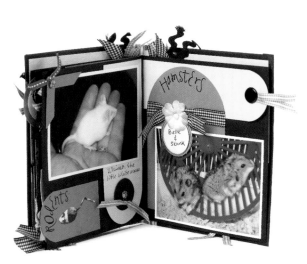

Why I Love Dogs by Irma Gabbard

Do the expressions on your dogs' faces make your heart melt? Irma Gabbard is so captivated by her pets' animated and expressive looks that she created an adorable album to remember them.

How To:

Decorate the cover of a blank board book, then design the interior pages using a similar format for each layout. Print and adhere journaling, along with photos, rubber-stamped images and rub-ons.

Irma's Tip:

Let a book inspire you. I found a publication on dogs with some wonderful photos and decided to make my own following a similar format. Try it with a book on any topic!

Supplies *Patterned paper:* Autumn Leaves; *Canvas frame, bubble letters, safety pins and ribbon:* Li'l Davis Designs; *Metal mesh and metal heart:* Making Memories; *Rub-on elements and book tape:* 7gypsies; *Rub-on letters:* KI Memories; *Rubber stamp:* B-Line Designs; *Transparency:* Autumn Leaves; *Brads:* Doodlebug Design; *Labels:* me & my BIG ideas; *Computer font:* Courier, Microsoft Word; *Other:* Board book.

Building a Dream Home **by Jennifer Gallacher**

Because Jennifer Gallacher is fascinated with home design, she keeps a stash of photos, paint chips and idea books on hand when she embarks on a new project. Her album is filled with home textiles and keeps track of wishes, ideas and inspiration.

How To:

Cover a chipboard album with patterned paper and embellishments. Decorate the album pages with patterned paper, stickers and other accents, then add appropriate embellishments to each layout, such as paint chips for a page on paint colors.

Jennifer's Tip:

When creating an album about your home or decorating projects, use embellishments that evoke the feeling of "home," such as floral patterned paper, tool charms, metal accents and more.

COVER
Supplies *Chipboard album, red stitched ribbon, chipboard frame, bookplate and home sticker:* Li'l Davis Designs; *Patterned papers:* Daisy D's Paper Co., Chatterbox, Karen Foster Design and Li'l Davis Designs; *Tool charms and paper floss:* Karen Foster Design; *Rub-on letters:* Making Memories; *Blue stitched ribbon:* C.M. Offray & Son; *Brads:* Junkitz.

INSPIRE ME
Supplies *Patterned papers:* Karen Foster Design, Li'l Davis Designs and Chatterbox; *Keyhole charm, epoxy stickers and epoxy frames:* Li'l Davis Designs; *Chipboard tags:* Making Memories; *Ribbon:* C.M. Offray & Son; *Brad:* Karen Foster Design.

PAINT OPTIONS
Supplies *Patterned papers:* Li'l Davis Designs and Karen Foster Design; *Textured cardstock:* Bazzill Basics Paper; *Burgundy ribbon, epoxy sticker, epoxy frame, house sticker and chipboard letter:* Li'l Davis Designs; *Jump ring and rub-on letters:* Making Memories; *Mini brads:* Karen Foster Design.

CONTRACTORS
Supplies *Patterned papers:* Karen Foster Design, Li'l Davis Designs and Chatterbox; *Label tag:* Carolee's Creations; *Epoxy stickers:* Li'l Davis Designs; *Brad and clear pocket:* Karen Foster Design; *Photo corners:* Canson; *"X" and "Q" labels:* Autumn Leaves; *Other:* Paper clips.

Dia de los Muertos
a community celebrates

MARIGOLD

Dia de los Muertos **by Linda Rodriguez**

Celebrate your culture and community with an album that highlights its most meaningful traditions. To help educate others about the annual Dia de los Muertos celebrations, Linda Rodriguez designed a colorful mini book to display during the festivities and help promote the event.

How To:

Use letter stickers to design titles for each section of the album. Add photos and embellishments to the pages, keeping the designs and backgrounds simple. Handwrite journaling throughout the book offering descriptions and explanations for each photo.

Linda's Tip:

If your photos are extremely colorful, try keeping your backgrounds simple. A mostly white base, for example, helps keep the photos the center of attention.

DIA DE LOS MUERTOS: A COMMUNITY CELEBRATES
Supplies *Album, cardstock and patterned paper:* Die Cuts With a View; *Letter stickers:* Doodlebug Design; *Leather flower, decorative brad, mini brad and flower charm:* Making Memories; *Flower punches:* EK Success; *Stamping ink:* Ranger Industries; *Pen:* Sharpie, Sanford; *Square brads:* Jo-Ann Scrap Essentials; *Other:* Twill and staples.

My Childhood Community **by Robyn Werlich**

Don't think "traditional" albums leave enough room for photos and memorabilia? Try Robyn Werlich's idea—use a large envelope as the "album cover," then fill it with smaller envelopes to serve as "pages." Whenever she remembers something about her childhood community, she slips a note into one of the envelopes along with photos and other tidbits.

How To:

Decorate a large envelope. Gather and embellish 10–12 smaller envelopes that will slip inside and serve as the "pages." Decorate each envelope with photos of a specific location in your community. Keep blank index cards or cardstock scraps with the envelopes for jotting notes and journaling as desired, then place them in the corresponding envelope.

Robyn's Tip:

When designing a project with envelopes, don't do anything that will prevent you from slipping items into them. For example, machine-stitch accents or add brads before adhering the pieces to the front of the envelopes.

Supplies *Envelope:* Paper Source; *Rub-ons, rhinestones, paper tags and brads:* Making Memories; *Plastic letters, rub-on letters and photo corners:* Heidi Swapp for Advantus; *Die-cut letters:* QuickKutz; *Other:* Paper clips, buttons, marker, ribbon and thread.

my
CHILDHOOD
COMMUNITY

remember when

Dodge City **by Nichol Magouirk**

Where do you live today? What do you love about it? Which details will you cherish years from now? Featuring photos of family, historical elements and landmarks, Nichol Magouirk's community album serves as a reminder of what they love about the city and documents interesting changes as years go by.

How To:

Create the inside pages using coordinating patterned paper and cardstock. Add journaling strips to each layout, then embellish with tags, brads, photo corners and chipboard letters. Decorate the cover with letters, a fabric pocket, a tag and dried flowers.

Nichol's Tip:

For graphic appeal, consider using photos that cover the entire width of the page. For my 8" x 8" album, for example, I used photos that were 8" wide for a clean look.

Supplies *Album:* QVC; *Patterned paper, die cuts, cardstock and ribbon:* KI Memories; *Tags and fabric pocket:* Making Memories; *Mini brads, photo corners and chipboard letter:* Heidi Swapp for Advantus; *Die-cut label:* Sizzix, Provo Craft; *Dried flowers:* Pressed Petals; *Computer font:* Avant Garde, downloaded from the Internet.

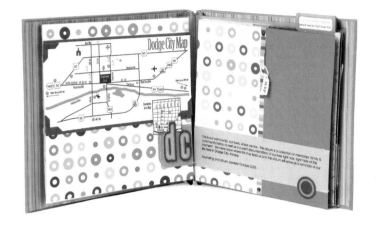

WWW.CREATINGKEEPSAKES.COM

Girls' Trip **by Shelley Laming**

To celebrate friendships, Shelley Laming devised a cute board book to gather the best photos and memories from a recent girls' trip. The project serves as a reminder of the fun times they had, and Shelley can turn to it time and again when she's missing her community of friends.

How To:

Adhere patterned paper to the front and back covers of a small board book. Adhere photos with adhesive dots. Distress patterned paper and letter stickers with stamping ink, then add them to the pages. Write your journaling and tie the book closed with ribbon.

Shelley's Tip:

When designing your pages, make sure you don't place anything too close to the inside (near the book's spine) or it will be too difficult to close the book.

Supplies *Patterned papers:* My Mind's Eye and Scenic Route Paper Co.; *Letter stickers:* Doodlebug Design; *Stamping ink:* ColorBox Fluid Chalk, Clearsnap; *Ribbon:* May Arts; *Pen:* Zig Millennium, EK Success; *Other:* Board book.

STUVWXYZ 123456789

PREPARING

FOR COLLEGE

- ✓ Do well on the ACT (35)
- ✓ Do well on the SAT (800 in Physics and Math) ☆
- ✓ Study hard (3.87 GPA)
- ✓ Submit applications to Darmouth, Columbia, U-Penn & Univ. of Chicago
- Locate a wealthy benefactor who wants to put a cute, smart kid through college

ABCDEFGHIJKLMNOPQR

Paint Your World

by Jennifer Purdie

Acrylic paints are a fun and easy way to add a splash of color to any scrapbook page. And since they dry quickly and are available in a rainbow of colors, you'll love how versatile they are. Whether you're new to acrylic paints or a seasoned pro, here are some tips for getting the most from this multipurpose item:

• Acrylic paints dry quickly, so any paint left on the outside of the bottle will dry out. To prevent paint from drying before you are finished working with it, keep a spray bottle nearby as you work. A fine spray of water will keep the paint moist.

• Keep a jar of water nearby as you paint, and rinse your brushes frequently. The paint will quickly dry in the bristles, and once it has dried, it's nearly impossible to remove.

• Although most acrylic paints aren't translucent, you can still use them to create a watercolor look—just add a little water. You'll still have the fast-drying quality of acrylic paints but with the lighter, lucid look of watercolors.

• If you're creating a collage, you can also use acrylic paint as glue. Be sure to use a generous amount (and make sure the paper isn't too thick).

• You can use acrylic paints on several mediums. For variation, apply acrylic paint over metal or wood embellishments, or paint the edges of a picture for a one-of-a-kind frame.

Be creative. The opportunities to use acrylic paints on your scrapbook pages are limitless!

gifts

What do you give the person who has everything? Put down the gift cards, pick up your supplies and browse through our one-stop shop of one-of-a-kind gifts. What would your loved one love best? A biographical scrapbook? A gorgeous piece of jewelry? A DVD of the year's highlights? Ensure she'll receive something that suits her taste, interests and personality by creating it yourself! Check out the projects in this chapter that demonstrate how a little personalization goes a long way when giving the perfect gift.

KEYCHAIN  **by Terri Davenport**

Need an inexpensive, quick gift for everyone on your list? With a small photo, a monogram and a few embellishments, the one designed by Terri Davenport would be a perfect, thoughtful trinket for teachers, neighbors and friends.

How To:

Find a thin wooden tag at your local craft store (ideally with a pre-punched hole). Decorate the tag with rubber-stamped, embossed images, patterned paper, stickers and more. Add ribbon and a beaded chain or a key ring.

Terri's Tip:

When decorating your tag with rubber-stamped images, try heat-embossing the images for dimension and greater staying power.

Supplies *Letter stickers and wood tag:* Chatterbox; *Letter stamps:* Hero Arts; *Stamping ink:* Brilliance, Tsukineko; *Decorative tape:* Gin-X, Imagination Project; *Ribbon:* May Arts; *Other:* Embossing powder.

COLLAGE NECKLACE The Joy of Motherhood **by Katherine Brooks**

Katherine Brooks turned her collage work into wearable art—and the perfect present for friends and family. Try showcasing altered artwork, scrapbook pages, art journal pages, photos and more in a small but stunning format.

How To:

Start your design by creating a collage on two pieces of 4" x 6" cardstock. Scan the artwork and reduce it to fit inside the glass. Print onto photo paper. Cut and attach the pieces together, back to back. Slip the artwork between the two pieces of glass and solder per soldering rod instructions. Add a jump ring, spiral clip and bead, then hang on a necklace chain.

Katherine's Tip:

Before soldering, consider taking a class and learning the basics to make it easier. Websites such as *www.scrapalatte.com* also offer helpful tips.

Supplies *Patterned papers:* Sweetwater, K&Company, Rusty Pickle and Daisy D's Paper Co.; *Letter stickers:* Pebbles Inc. and Creative Imaginations; *Soldering supplies:* Scrap a Latte; *Spiral clip and gaffer tape:* 7gypsies; *Stamping ink:* Ranger Industries; *Water-soluble wax pastels:* Caran d'Ache; *Computer font:* 39 Smooth, downloaded from the Internet; *Other:* Bead, jump rings and necklace.

Charm Bracelet by Tracey Odachowski

Give grandparents, friends or even yourself a bracelet that's not only beautiful, but meaningful, too. According to Tracey Odachowski, only pliers were required to create this piece, which features a handmade photo charm and can be custom-made in any color.

How To:

Cut three lengths of tigertail. Attach clasp and crimp. Thread beads, alternating among the three strands. Print two photos approximately ¾" in diameter and trim. Pour epoxy over one photo and allow to dry. Then pour a small amount of epoxy on the back of the photo and place a second image—face up—on top. Pour epoxy over the top. Before completely set, use a paper piercer to make a hole in the top of the charm. Use a jump ring to attach the charm to the bracelet.

Tracey's Tip:

Don't be intimidated—making a piece of jewelry is really easy. If you'd rather not create the epoxy charm, use a metal or pre-printed charm, or a find a charm frame and simply slip a photo inside.

Supplies *Beads:* Hirschberg Schutz & Co.; *Silver tigertail, clasps and crimps:* Halcraft; *Jump rings:* Beadalon.

PHOTO SHIRT

TML by Kate Teague

Want to share your favorite scrapbook pages with family and friends? Why not present them with keepsake T-shirts that feature your most meaningful and eye-catching pages? Kate Teague kept the focus on the photo for her project, a gift that celebrates the special bond her sister and daughter share.

How To:
Design a layout digitally. Print the page onto iron-on transfer paper, then iron the page onto a plain white T-shirt.

Kate's Tip:
You can also transfer scrapbook pages onto items like pillowcases, sheets and curtains. Be sure to wash the piece carefully, however, to preserve the transfer.

Supplies *Stitching:* Kristie David, downloaded from *www.theshabbyshoppe.com;* *Floral border:* Kate Teague, downloaded from *www.designerdigitals.com;* *All other accents:* A2Z Essentials.

PLATE FRAME

Ethan by Leah LaMontagne

A ceramic plate and a length of ribbon serve as the perfect "frame" for a cherished photo. Consider creating a similar display for a wedding or baby gift—with letter stamps and solvent ink, the ribbon "message" can be customized to suit any photo.

How To:
Stamp letters onto ribbon. Weave the ribbon through the notches in the plate, then add brads. Cut your photo into a circle, ink the edges and adhere it to the center of the plate.

Leah's Tip:
If you can't find a plate with a notched rim, just add ribbon to a regular plate with a hot glue gun.

Supplies *Ribbon:* Li'l Davis Designs; *Rubber stamps:* Technique Tuesday; *Stamping ink:* StazOn, Tsukineko; *Mini brads:* Making Memories; *Other:* Ceramic plate.

WWW.CREATINGKEEPSAKES.COM

April by Leah LaMontagne

What mother wouldn't treasure a photo plaque of her baby? Leah LaMontagne used texture paste and a large monogram as part of a design that also includes two adorable photos. Customize the gift further with the baby's name, age and a special message on the back.

How To:
Paint the plaque and monogram with acrylic paint. Add paint to molding paste to achieve the colors you want to appear raised. Smear paste over a flower and leaf stencil with a craft spatula. After the paste is dry, remove the stencil. Adhere the photos to cardboard (for durability) and attach to the background with dimensional foam tape. Hot-glue the pieces in place.

Leah's Tip:
Molding paste is a great medium for creating dimensional looks. You only need one tub. Mix with acrylic paint for custom colors or add glitter, dried flower pieces and more for additional effects.

Supplies *Monogram:* Provo Craft; *Acrylic paint:* Plaid Enterprises; *3-D molding paste:* American Traditional Designs; *Ribbon:* Michaels; *Acrylic letters:* Jo-Ann Scrap Essentials; *Stencil:* Delta Technical Coatings; *Other:* Wooden plaque.

Friends by Shannon Taylor

Give your best friend a whimsical photo housed in a cute, custom-decorated license plate frame like Shannon Taylor's. Choose ribbon to coordinate with your photo or use colors that correspond with the gift—white for a wedding photo, pastels for a baby or brights for a teen.

How To:
Paint and chalk chipboard letters and attach them to a license plate frame. Tie ribbon around the rest of the frame and add charms with jump rings. Attach a photo to the back with double-stick tape for sturdiness.

Shannon's Tip:
Start with a darker license plate frame; if a bit of it shows through the embellishments, the darker color won't be as noticeable as white or silver.

Supplies *License plate:* Advanced Auto Parts; *Ribbon:* Li'l Davis Designs, C.M. Offray & Son and unknown; *Jump rings:* Junkitz; *Heart charms:* Delight; Maude and Millie; *Heart stickpin:* Nunn Design; *Chipboard letters and acrylic paint:* Making Memories; *Double-sided tape:* Therm O Web; *Other:* Decorative chalks.

Family Photo Shoot by Tena Sprenger

After taking photos of her brother's family before they moved out of state, Tena Sprenger knew coasters adorned with those images would be the perfect housewarming gift. Because the project is quick and easy, the coasters would also make great bonus gifts for professional photographers to present to clients.

How To:

Crop four photos to the same size as marble coasters. Print images onto transfer paper using a color laser printer. Follow the manufacturer's instructions to transfer the images onto the coasters.

Tena's Tip:

Selecting high-contrast photos to transfer will give you better results and allow more detail to show through. Follow the package instructions carefully to avoid mistakes.

Supplies *Marble coaster kit:* Tilano Fresco; *Transfer paper:* Color Lazer Printer.

Daddy's Little Girls by Shannon Zickel

Shannon Zickel knew a handmade keepsake would be the perfect solution for a Father's Day gift. She designed a photo collage, a meaningful creation that's elegant, yet masculine enough to display on the wall of her father's office.

How To:

Using a square punch, punch out 21 photos and three coordinating pieces of patterned paper. Mount the photos in three rows, placing one block of patterned paper in each row. Add accents and a title. Place the completed project in a 12" x 24" frame.

Shannon's Tip:

If you have a large-format printer, you can create a montage with photo-editing software and print it directly onto the background paper to eliminate the need for punching and measuring.

Supplies *Patterned papers:* Scenic Route Paper Co.; *Chipboard hearts and letters:* Heidi Swapp for Advantus; *Rub-ons:* Making Memories; *Square punch:* Marvy Uchida; *Other:* Frame.

Stephanie by Candace Stringham

Do you have a sibling who's also a great friend? Show her how much you appreciate and cherish your relationship with an album like the one Candace Stringham designed for her sister, a children's book author. For added meaning, allow the book's feel to reflect the subject's career, tastes and interests.

How To:

Cut museum board to size and create frames with a craft knife. Sew patterned paper together and affix to the background. Brainstorm about the things your subject enjoys and incorporate them into the design of each layout.

Candace's Tip:

When working with museum board, make clean cuts by using a craft knife and straight edge. Change the blade often to keep cuts crisp.

Supplies *Software:* Adobe Photoshop Elements, Adobe Systems; *Custom brushes:* Rhonna Farrer; *Patterned papers:* Scenic Route Paper Co., Chatterbox, Autumn Leaves, My Mind's Eye and Making Memories; *Vellum:* American Crafts; *Textured cardstock:* Bazzill Basics Paper; *Jewels:* Heidi Swapp for Advantus; *Ribbon:* American Crafts; *Acrylic paint, paper flowers and rub-ons:* Making Memories; *Computer fonts:* 2Peas Civilian, 2Peas Organic and 2Peas Red Velvet Cake, downloaded from *www.twopeasinabucket.com*; *Other:* Museum board, book cloth, transparency, thread, jewel brad and silk flowers.

WWW.CREATINGKEEPSAKES.COM

A True Friend
by Linda Rodriguez

- Karen, 1975
- Priscilla, 1978
- Audra, 1983
- Chela, 1986
- Jennifer, 1988
- Gwynetta, 1990
- Katherine, 2002
- Gabrielle, 2003
- Stacy, Barb, Susan, Amber, 2005

Don't walk behind me; I may not lead.
Don't walk in front of me; I may not follow.
Just walk beside me and be my friend.
~Albert Camus

You've got a friend in me.

Karen, 1975

A true friend lets you be the princess.

A true friend reaches for your hand and touches your heart. ~Kathee Coleman

Chela, 1986

A true friend takes College Calculus with you just for FUN!

The best way to mend a broken heart is time and girlfriends.
~Gwyneth Paltrow

A true friend knows how to make you smile even when you don't feel like it.

Jennifer, 1988

Pay tribute to the friends you've had in your life. Linda Rodriguez tied her album together with coordinating materials and journaling tidbits that each begin with the phrase "A True Friend ..." Consider asking your group of friends to design a mini book with a page about each member, then swapping albums at a gift exchange!

How To:
Cut chipboard covers and cardstock pages. Create cardstock "hinges" to attach the pages, accordion style. Affix ribbon to the cover to tie the book closed. Add photos, journaling and accents to each page. Decorate the cover with rub-ons, punched flowers and other embellishments.

Linda's Tip:
Coordinated paper and embellishments can give the book a more unified look, but when designing an accordion album, don't worry too much about the scrapbook pages "matching" the page on the other side.

Supplies *Textured cardstock:* Die Cuts With a View; *Patterned papers, acrylic accents and ribbon:* KI Memories; *Rub-ons:* Scrapworks; *Flower and circle punches:* EK Success; *Stamping ink:* Stampabilities; *Mini flower brads and silver brads:* Making Memories; *Pen:* Sharpie, Sanford; *Other:* Chipboard, buttons and staples.

a true friend

Grandma's Brag Box   by Miley Johnson

Here's the perfect gift for grandparents who love to take photos of the grandkids—a decorated, archival photo box. Miley Johnson completed hers with decorated dividers for each child and pretty adornments that will make it a welcome addition to her mother's home decor.

How To:

Purchase a plain photo box and envelopes. Cover the box with patterned paper and ribbon. Decorate each envelope, adding photos and name tags. Embellish the inside with photos, patterned paper and accents.

Miley's Tip:

Since the box will be opened and shut a lot, be sure to use a good adhesive for durability. I made sure everything was dry and secure before I added the ribbon and other accents.

Supplies *Patterned papers:* K&Company and 7gypsies; *Ribbon:* May Arts, Making Memories and SEI; *Chipboard triangle:* Bazzill Basics Paper; *Wooden letters:* Li'l Davis Designs; *Photo box and photo envelopes:* Archiver's; *Letter stamps:* Hero Arts; *Elastic:* 7gypsies; *Brads:* Karen Foster Design; *Metal letters:* Making Memories; *Computer font:* 2Peas Evergreen, downloaded from *www.twopeasinabucket.com.*

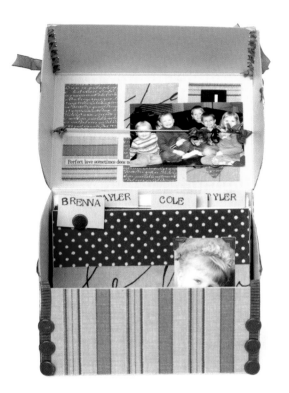

Altered Boxes
by Jennifer Purdie

Altered boxes are a great way to personalize gifts, and they're perfect for storing scrapbooking supplies, trinkets and more. Plus, you likely have all the supplies you need right in your scrapbooking stash! Here's how to create these cool containers:

Supplies:

Box of any size	Decoupage medium
Patterned paper	Waxed paper
Scissors	Small sponge

Step 1: Find or purchase a plain box.

Step 2: Remove any tags, tape, stamps, etc.

Step 3: Paint the entire box with one coat of acrylic paint in the color of your choice. This will help the decoupage medium stick to the surface better and creates a nice, clean base for your patterned paper. If your box is lighter-weight, such as a hat or shoe box, cover it with copy paper instead of paint (the paint will be too heavy).

Step 4: Cut your patterned paper into 2" or larger squares.

Step 5: Place your box on waxed paper (which will prevent adhesive from sticking to your workspace). Decide how you want to lay out your patterned paper. Try different styles and arrangements until you find what you like best.

Step 6: Using a small sponge, coat the edges of the patterned-paper squares with decoupage medium and adhere to the box, starting on the bottom. Be sure to smooth out any wrinkles.

Step 7: Wrap the squares of patterned paper around the rim of the box and under the lid. Smooth everything flat so the lid will fit.

Step 8: When the outside of the box is complete, begin decorating the inside. Score the squares along the top of the box and inside the crease of the lid. Trim any excess and press the edges into place.

Step 9: Coat the box, both inside and out, with decoupage medium and let dry.

John Cole by Sam Cole

As a surprise for his brother's birthday, Sam Cole created an 8" x 8" album that looks back at 30 memorable years. Packed with nostalgic family photos, memories and meaningful song lyrics, a walk down memory lane like this would also make a great retirement gift!

How To:

Complete scrapbook pages to represent various time periods throughout the recipient's life. Add interest by going back and forth between simple and more advanced scrapbook pages throughout the album, always keeping the focus on the photos.

Sam's Tip:

Since smaller albums can't hold as much "stuff," it's important to fill the album with the most meaningful photos first.

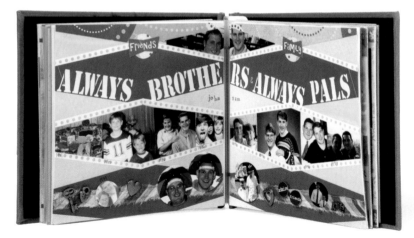

Supplies *Textured cardstock and chipboard:* Bazzill Basics Paper; *Patterned papers:* Kopp Design, K&Company, Creative Imaginations, Chatterbox, Anna Griffin, Sandylion, Frances Meyer, Autumn Leaves, EK Success and KI Memories; *Frame, photo corners and metal word:* Making Memories; *Letter stickers:* Mustard Moon, Creative Imaginations, American Crafts, Wordsworth, Sandylion, Li'l Davis Designs and Pebbles Inc.; *Metal art and epoxy stickers:* K&Company; *"Friend" accent:* My Mind's Eye; *Sports stickers:* Creative Memories and Paper House Productions; *Woven labels:* me & my BIG ideas; *Circle and heart punches:* EK Success; *Letter stamps:* Hero Arts; *Rubber stamp:* 100 Proof Press; *Stamping ink:* Clearsnap and Tsukineko; *Ribbon:* SEI and C.M. Offray & Son; *Rub-ons:* Autumn Leaves; *Acrylic paint:* Plaid Enterprises; *Star punch:* Emagination Crafts; *Buttons:* Li'l Davis Designs; *Pen:* Zig Millennium, EK Success; *"Journey" stickers:* Karen Foster Design; *White brad:* All Sorts of Things; *Circle punch:* Punch Bunch; *Dot rubber stamp:* Savvy Stamps.

friend

a gift

imagine

JOHN COLE

FATHER

Leader

SPIRIT

WHAT A GUY!

THE 30 1st YRS.

WWW.CREATINGKEEPSAKES.COM

Kindergarten Rulz **by Miley Johnson**

Get the students involved in creating a gift every teacher will love. As a present for her son's kindergarten teacher, Miley Johnson asked each student a question and included their answers and photos on the pages of a cute, spiral-bound book. Because of the small size, the project was fast to create, yet filled with meaning.

How To:

Cut strips of paper to the same size as a ruler to use as the pages for the album. Take the strips to a copy center to be coil-bound. Paint the ruler (which will become the cover), and decorate as desired. Glue the ruler to the front of the album with liquid adhesive. Add photos and accents to pages, then decorate the spine with ribbon.

Miley's Tip:

The ruler motif can easily be modified for other types of albums, like a "look how they grow" grandparents' album or a book highlighting each year of school.

Supplies *Patterned papers:* Making Memories and Die Cuts With a View; *Rub-ons:* Making Memories; *Ribbon:* 7gypsies and C.M. Offray & Son; *Ruler:* Wal-Mart; *Binding:* FedEx Kinko's.

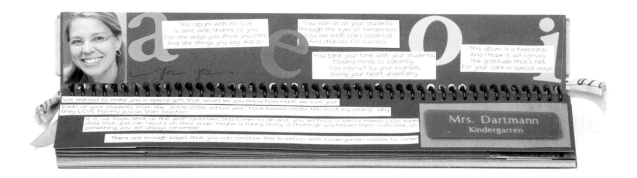

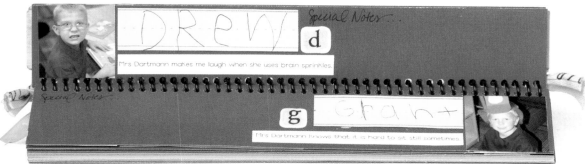

WWW.CREATINGKEEPSAKES.COM

Father's Day Treats by Darcee Waddoups

For the man who has everything, follow Darcee Waddoup's example and create a Father's Day candy holder that gives him a snack, family photos and a reminder you love him all at the same time. By using a large spice rack, you can supply a generous amount of memories and sweets!

How To:

Purchase a spice rack. Remove the spices and wash jars thoroughly. Use a circle punch to trim photos for the lids. Adhere the photos and seal with clear glaze. Cut patterned paper for the labels and decorate before affixing to the jars. Decorate the rack and fill the jars with candy.

Darcee's Tip:

Practice with scrap paper to measure and get the right size to cover the jars and the rack itself (the area with the holes can be tricky). This way, you won't ruin a lot of expensive patterned paper!

Supplies *Patterned paper:* Scenic Route Paper Co.; *Letter stickers:* SEI, The C-Thru Ruler Co., Wordsworth, Boxer Scrapbook Productions and Colorbök; *Rub-ons and brad:* Making Memories; *Stamping ink:* StazOn, Tsukineko and Making Memories; *Rubber stamps:* Carolee's Creations, Hero Arts and Toyoda Multi Joint; *Clear glaze:* Mod Podge, Plaid Enterprises; *Spice rack:* Mainstays, Wal-Mart; *Circle punch:* McGill; *Pens:* Sakura and American Crafts; *Other:* Thread and buttons.

Recipes by Tracy Miller

Tracy Miller fashioned a homespun addition to any cookbook shelf—a decorated folder to hold recipes and more. A decorative way to gather all the recipes for a holiday meal, family standards or dishes you'd like to try, this project is a perfect neighbor, shower or housewarming gift.

How To:

Punch a hole in the chipboard for a fastener, then attach the chipboard to the front of a photo file. Create a title with foam stamps and chipboard letters. Attach the title strip to the cover and add a tag behind it. Attach patterned paper to the inside of the file and adorn with decorated tabs.

Tracy's Tip:

Although these index files are made to hold photos, they can be adapted for other projects. Use preprinted backgrounds and accents to make a simple project look like it took a lot of time to create!

Supplies *Patterned paper, chipboard letters, foam stamps, and background and strips:* Li'l Davis Designs; *Letter stamps:* PSX Design; *Circle tabs and tag:* Déjà Views, The C-Thru Ruler Co.; *Rub-ons:* Autumn Leaves; *Pen:* Pigment Pro, American Crafts.

WWW.CREATINGKEEPSAKES.COM

Jewelry Boxes **by Candace Leonard**

When giving a gift, make it even more special with a customized box. Try designs like these by Candace Leonard that incorporate a photo or monogram for that extra-special someone. Or tailor the colors to match the recipient's home decor so the box can hold knickknacks once empty.

How To:
Purchase boxes of various sizes from the craft store. Cover with patterned paper and die cuts using decoupage medium. Once dry, embellish with photos, rub-ons, flowers and ribbon pulls.

Candace's Tip:
Allow plenty of time for the decoupage medium to dry between coats, and use a brayer to help smooth any air bubbles between the paper and box.

Supplies *Patterned papers, die cuts and rub-on:* KI Memories; *Ribbon:* American Crafts; *Acrylic paint and decorative tape:* Heidi Swapp for Advantus; *Rubber stamps:* Postmodern Design; *Stamping ink:* Memories, Stewart Superior Corporation; *Decoupage medium:* Mod Podge, Plaid Enterprises.

I Love You **by Jennifer Gallacher**

What mom doesn't deserve a bit of pampering? Jennifer Gallacher created a personalized spa treatment in a box for her mother, complete with photos of the grandchildren. It's a gift and memento rolled into one. Once the bath products are removed, the decorated box can house more photos or memorabilia from the children.

How To:
Cover the lid of a box with acrylic paint, patterned paper, cardstock and accents. Gently peel labels from shampoo and bath gel bottles and replace with decorated tags and charms hung with floss. Hand-stitch a clear bag from a transparency and fill with potpourri.

Jennifer's Tip:
Covering a dimensional item with patterned paper can be difficult. I traced the outline of the object onto the back of the paper, then trimmed to fit. Use ribbon to cover any mistakes!

COVER
Supplies *Patterned paper:* Chatterbox; *Ribbon:* Li'l Davis Designs; *Acrylic paint:* Delta Technical Coatings; *Rub-ons:* Déjà Views, The C-Thru Ruler Co.; *Metal-rimmed tags:* Making Memories; *Circle cutter:* Lighthouse Memories; *Jumbo scallop scissors:* Fiskars; *Other:* Box and transparency.

GIFTS
Supplies *Patterned paper and ribbon:* Li'l Davis Designs; *Metal word charms and paper floss:* Karen Foster Design; *Other:* Shampoo and bath gel.

GREETING CARD BOX

Cards by Vicki Harvey

A container designed by Vicki Harvey is just right for organizing cards you plan to send or storing sentimental ones you'd like to keep. Try creating a box as a wedding or baby shower gift and filling it with store-bought "thank you" cards, a pen and stamps.

How To:

Purchase a plain box. Embellish with patterned paper, ribbon, chipboard letters and flowers. Decorate divider cards with paper, ribbon and accents. Add an index tab to the top of each divider with the name of the card category.

Vicki's Tip:

If the pre-printed index tabs don't have titles to fit your categories, simply print them on cardstock, then trim to fit inside the tabs.

Supplies *Patterned papers:* Melissa Frances, Daisy D's Paper Co., Mustard Moon, We R Memory Keepers, Chatterbox, K&Company, The C-Thru Ruler Co., Reminisce, Bo-Bunny Press, All My Memories and Anna Griffin; *Ribbon:* C.M. Offray & Son, May Arts and Impress Rubber Stamps; *Flowers:* Michaels; *Acrylic paint, brad, plaque, button, metal-rimmed tag and white lace:* Making Memories; *Watch face:* Li'l Davis Designs; *Chipboard letters:* BasicGrey; *Index tabs:* Heidi Swapp for Advantus; *Epoxy sticker:* Colorbök; *Birthday cake die cut:* K&Company; *White tags:* Avery; *Rub-on stocking:* Daisy D's Paper Co.; *Green, blue and pink sticker and "Boo" sticker:* Reminisce; *Rose die cut:* Anna Griffin; *Green polka-dot tag:* All My Memories; *Black letter stickers:* Creative Memories; *Twill:* Wrights; *Computer font:* 2Peas Evergreen, downloaded from www.twopeasinabucket.com; *Other* Vintage rickrack.

PHOTO BOX

Doodads by Teri Fode

If the next person on your gift list collects trinkets, photos or doodads, present her with a decorated box to store her treasured pieces. Teri Fode designed this box as a little gift for a friend to hold small craft supplies like flowers, ribbon and sewing notions.

How To:

Purchase a photo storage box and remove the metal label holder. Measure and cut patterned paper to fit the sides and top of the box. Paint a think coat of liquid adhesive on the box, then immediately adhere the patterned paper. Adorn the box with accents that coordinate with your theme.

Teri's Tip:

Be sure to measure and score the edges of each section of patterned paper since one 12" x 12" sheet will have to be "pieced" to fit a normal photo box.

Supplies *Box and silk flowers:* Michaels; *Patterned papers and monograms:* BasicGrey; *Paper flowers:* Prima and Making Memories; *Ribbon and pins:* Making Memories; *Jewels:* The Card Connection; *Pen:* American Crafts; *Monogram card:* K&Company; *Other:* Buttons.

| CREATING KEEPSAKES

CREATIVE KEEPSALES

Grandpa's Biggest Fans

by Laurie Stamas

Because her father lives out of state and doesn't see his grandchildren very often, Laurie Stamas designed an interactive DVD scrapbook to keep him up to date. Since it features a movie of each child that includes photos, videos of their activities and taped interviews, the project is the ideal way to share with long-distance family and friends.

How To:

Use sturdy chipboard to create the album pages. Decorate the pages with patterned paper, photos and accents. Attach a CD envelope to the back of each photo page and add the subject's name to the flap. Place a DVD inside each envelope. Connect the pages with a metal post, ribbon or key rings.

Laurie's Tip:

If you don't own the software to create movies or your computer isn't equipped with a DVD-ROM drive, consider burning photos to a CD that the recipient can watch like a slide show.

Supplies *Software:* MemoryMixer, Lasting Impressions for Paper; *Patterned paper:* BasicGrey; *Plastic letters:* Artistic Expressions; *Printed twill and metal corners:* 7gypsies; *Silver jump rings and page pebbles:* Making Memories; *Rub-ons:* Making Memories, 7gypsies and Autumn Leaves; *Black jump rings:* Junkitz; *Pen:* Slick Writer, American Crafts; *Letter stickers:* Cavallini & Co.; *Metal clips:* Wal-Mart; *CD envelopes:* OfficeMax; *Other:* Metal post from a post-bound album and pre-cut chipboard pieces.

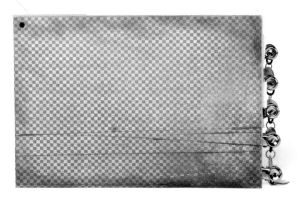

ALTERED CD COVERS

Gift Covers *by Joy Uzarraga*

As an annual tradition, send photos or video footage of your family to long-distance relatives. Make the gift even more significant by sprucing up plain cases with photos and other embellishments that represent the month, year or season.

How To:

Create CD covers by using photo-editing software, or adhere patterned paper, photos and embellishments to cardstock measuring 4¾" x 4¾" (the size of a CD jewel case). Create the DVD cover by trimming white cardstock to wrap around the front and back. Adhere photos and strips of patterned paper to the front. Print the DVD's year and title and affix to the front and spine.

Joy's Tip:

Consider using themed patterned papers or elements from the same manufacturer that will take the guess-work out of mixing and matching.

Supplies *Patterned papers:* Sweetwater; *Computer fonts:* Century Gothic and Monotype Corporation, downloaded from the Internet.

June - watermelon
g, summer parties - J
- June -- cool summe
eques- June - hot do
valks in the park. kids pla
nshine, kisses- June -
. vacations, barbeques-

mmer '05

january   january   januar
February

March M
april

June - ho
days, swimm
ne - water
nelon, sunshi

august august a
ust august augu

SEPTEMBER SEPTEMBER

October · October

november november november november november novemb
ober · Oct
october december december december

2005 2005 2005 2005 2005 2005 2005 2005 2005 2005

February
winter '05
january
january
january
january
januar
ary   janu
december december december december

SEPTEMBER
Aa Bb Cc Dd Ee Ff Gg Hh Ii Jj Kk Ll
SEPTEMBER
Aa Bb Cc Dd Ee Ff Gg Hh Ii Jj Kk Ll
autumn '05   SEPTEMBER
november november november no
October
ber · Oct
november november november novem
October

May
april
april
april
March March
spring '05
March
March March

WWW.CREATINGKEEPSAKES.COM

Picture Perfect by Melissa Chapman

When Melissa Chapman does a photo shoot, she loves to present the disc in a clever, personal manner. The decorative case—which would also be the perfect way to present photo CDs to family and friends—instantly displays a few of her favorite shots and makes the CD easily identifiable for clients as well.

How To:
Choose four photos, resize them and place them in a square formation. Trim the photos with a circle cutter and mat with patterned paper. Add title lettering.

Melissa's Tip:
You don't have to be "crafty" to create a unique disc cover. If you'd rather, just slip the photo circle into a plastic jewel case instead.

Supplies *Patterned paper and acrylic word:* KI Memories; *Textured cardstock:* Bazzill Basics Paper; *Computer fonts:* Amertype and Impact, downloaded from the Internet.

A Gift for You by Rhonna Farrer

Rather than duplicating or even re-creating scrapbook pages to share with family, scan and burn them to a compact disc instead. Rhonna Farrer compiled several scrapbook pages for her sister's birthday, along with photos and songs. Topped off with a custom-designed cover, it's an easy and eye-catching gift.

How To:
Create a compact disc cover using a digital scrapbooking kit. Burn digital scrapbook pages, photos or music to a CD. Print the CD cover and label, cut out and assemble.

Rhonna's Tip:
If you're adding the digitally designed cover to a jewel case, apply rub-ons, stickers or ribbon to the outside for a bit of dimension.

Supplies *Software:* Adobe Photoshop CS2, Adobe Systems; *Designing With Digital* Book/CD, Autumn Leaves; *Custom brushes:* Rhonna Farrer for Autumn Leaves; *Digital kit:* Black Eyed Pea, downloaded from *www.twopeasinabucket.com*.

There's Always Room for Leftovers
by Leslie Miller

It's inevitable. After you've completed a beautiful scrapbook layout or other keepsake, you're left with little scraps, leftover charms and the like. Before long, those little piles of "leftovers" grow into a mountain of what most people call trash. But don't throw out all those strips of patterned paper, small lengths of ribbon and trim, and leftover letters. Turn your trash into treasures by finding small projects to make your scraps shine! I created this mini album for my father-in-law with scraps of patterned paper and ribbon I had held onto "just in case" I needed them.

Use Your Scraps for These Easy Projects:

Mini albums

Handmade greeting cards

Gift tags

Door hangers

Collage-style projects

Small accents

Notebook covers

Decorative place cards

Designer note cards

Personalized envelopes

Gifts bags

Bonus Idea:

Use your "scraps" to explore new techniques. That way, you don't "waste" your new sheet of paper or piece of ribbon. It's the perfect way to discover which techniques you love and which you'd rather let someone else try.

The Things You've Handed Down

by Leslie Miller

Supplies *Patterned papers:* Chatterbox and Scenic Route Paper Co.; *Ribbon:* Chatterbox and Making Memories; *Rub-on letters:* Making Memories; *Pen:* Pigma Micron, Sakura.

home decor

It's your home ... an extension of your family, lifestyle and personality. What better way to spruce up the rooms than to feature decor that celebrates the events, relationships and love you share within them? It's easy to adorn your walls, organizational items and even clocks so they're not just pretty, but pretty meaningful.

If you're in the mood to give your home a little striking—and significant—decoration, study the following projects that are guaranteed to supply a roomful of ideas.

CHILDREN ARE AN HERITAGE TO THE LORD.

Photos **by Rhonna Farrer**

Give your mantel meaning with an appealing photo arrangement. Rhonna Farrer's home features an expressive display—altered photos and accents surround a vinyl wall quote that pays tribute to her sense of family. With a collection like this, photos can be changed easily as your family changes and grows.

How To:

Gather assorted photo frames. Use photo-editing software to alter the photos using text, brushes and other effects. Print the photos on different photo papers for a variety of looks. Assemble all the photos and place in the frames.

Rhonna's Tip:

Add interest to photo decor by customizing your photos. Add scriptures, quotes, names or dates along with custom brush designs using photo-editing software.

Supplies *Software:* Adobe Photoshop CS2, Adobe Systems; *Brushes, flowers and negative strip:* Peas & Harmony digital kit, Rhonna Farrer, downloaded from *www.twopeasinabucket.com; Transparency:* Graphix; *Computer fonts:* Times New Roman and Arial, Microsoft Word; Zothique, Scriptorium.com and Professor, downloaded from the Internet; AL Uncle Charles, downloaded from *www.two-peasinabucket.com.*

Quilts **by Allison Kimball**

Because quilting has been a part of Allison Kimball's life since her childhood, she wanted a place in her home to illustrate its significance. Using an antique ladder, she now has a way to not only showcase her favorite quilts, but also display photos of the crafters who created them.

How To:

Purchase or find an antique ladder and photo frames. Attach eyehooks to the ladder to hold the frames and hang the ladder on the wall. Tie the frames onto the hooks with ribbon. Paint letters and add to the ladder with metal brackets.

Allison's Tip:

Add as many or as few picture frames as you'd like, depending on how many quilts you'd like to display. If you have an antique quilt, be sure to track down a photo of the person who made it.

Supplies *Ladder:* From *www.rusticgarden.com; Ribbon:* Scrapworks; *Wooden "O":* Allison's own design; *Acrylic paint:* Making Memories; *Papier-mâché letters:* Provo Craft; *Eyehooks and metal bracket:* The Home Depot; *Other:* Picture frames.

| WWW.CREATINGKEEPSAKES.COM

Photo Hooks **by Kim Kesti**

If you want to showcase a lot of photos but don't have a lot of wall space, create a system similar to Kim Kesti's. Although the scrapbook pages in the hanging frames are small, the black-and-white photos and bold stripes make a dramatic impact.

How To:

Resize four photos to 3" x 4". Create mini scrapbook pages to fit within glass frames. Punch circles and use rub-on letters as monograms. Assemble the glass frames and hang them from hooks with ribbon.

Kim's Tip:

If you're short on time, use a patterned paper with a striped design to avoid cutting narrow strips of cardstock.

Supplies *Pegboard:* Target; *Ribbon:* Scrapworks and May Arts; *Rub-ons:* SEI; *Flower stamp:* Stampin' Up!; *Stamping ink:* StazOn, Tsukineko; *Glass frames with clips:* Ikea.

Halloween **by Jenni Bowlin**

Design an eye-catching garland for any season by hanging decorative shapes strung together with ribbon. Jenni Bowlin turned her Halloween garland into a family history showcase by adding pictures of her kids, her mother and herself in costumes.

How To:

Cut stars from chipboard. Cover some stars with patterned paper and the remaining stars with acrylic paint, adding dots with a round brush. Add photos to the center of each star, then embellish them with bookplates, stickers, ribbon, rub-ons and sequins. Connect the stars and hang with ribbon.

Jenni's Tip:

Be sure to use removable adhesive to hang your garland to protect the finish on your furniture or mantel.

Supplies *Patterned papers:* Li'l Davis Designs and Creative Imaginations; *Bookplates, black ribbon, epoxy letters and settings:* Li'l Davis Designs; *Rub-ons and stickers:* Making Memories; *Orange-and-black ribbon:* Jo-Ann Stores; *Acrylic paint:* Delta Technical Coatings; *Other:* Transparency, letter set, star sequins and chipboard.

WWW.CREATINGKEEPSAKES.COM

Family Keys **by Lana Rickabaugh**

Does your family's key collection resemble a valet parking board? Give the spot in your house a little personality by turning a plain board into a decorative seasonal display. With its interchangeable canvas panels, Lana Rickabaugh's key box can be transformed from season to season.

How To:

Sand the front panel of a key box and paint over any existing design. Create panels for each holiday on canvas. Drill holes in the opposite corners of the box and stretch elastic from corner to corner to hold the panels on the front.

Lana's Tip:

Consider using leftover wallet-sized school photos or have small prints made to fit on a small key box.

Supplies *Canvas panels:* Fredrix; *Patterned papers, bottle cap and stickers:* Design Originals; *Foam stamps:* Heidi Swapp for Advantus; *Acrylic paint:* Delta Technical Coatings; *Foam corner stamp and snowflake charms:* Making Memories; *Other:* Wooden key box, flower, bookplate and ribbon.

Book Frame **by Jenni Bowlin**

Inspired by an idea in a home-decorating magazine, Jenni Bowlin loved the result of her first try at a book photo frame. Though she chose one with a blank cover, try using a book with a printed title that coordinates with the theme of your photo.

How To:

Find a hardcover book at a used book or antique store. Place a bookplate on the cover where you'd like your picture to be and trace the center. Cut out the shape with a craft knife, then attach the bookplate with brads. Adhere the photo to the inside cover page so it's framed through the bookplate.

Jenni's Tip:

When choosing a book, look at the inside pages as well. The one I chose features a map on the first page that makes a great mat for the photo.

Supplies *Epoxy number and setting:* Li'l Davis Designs; *Rub-on star:* 7gypsies; *Other:* Vintage bookplate.

Photo Stand **by Christy Tomlinson**

Christy Tomlinson found a way to combine her loves of scrapbooking, crafting and photography: designing creative picture holders to showcase beloved photos. Because the candle holders are a blank canvas, you can tailor your designs to suit your decor, adding letters to spell out seasonal words and more.

How To:

Purchase unpainted candlestick holders. Paint the base of each candle and drill a hole through the center of the "cup" portion. Glue one end of a 12" piece of wire inside the hole and curl the other end with pliers. Glue moss in the center to hide the wire, then embellish.

Christy's Tip:

You can also use decorated candle holders to display cherished holiday cards you receive from friends and family.

Supplies *Patterned paper:* Chatterbox; *Ribbon:* May Arts and Chatterbox; *Paper flower:* Prima; *Rub-ons and acrylic paint:* Making Memories; *Other:* Craft wire, Spanish moss and wood candlestick holder.

By the Sea **by Jenni Bowlin**

Jenni Bowlin collects antique glass bottles but was stumped for ways to use the ones with thinner necks. Problem solved! A bit of sand, a few scraps and some small photos, and she's got a striking decoration for her scrap studio.

How To:

Find a bottle at a flea market or antique store. Print the desired photo on standard computer paper. Add sand to the bottle, then roll the photo slightly and insert it into the bottle. You can position the photo with long tweezers. Or simply adhere the photo directly to the bottle, then add stickers and text as embellishments.

Jenni's Tip:

Get creative when choosing the "filling" for your bottle. Try pumpkin seeds for fall, jelly beans for Easter or glitter for the holidays.

Supplies *Computer font:* Times New Roman, Microsoft Word; *Other:* Antique bottles, vintage rhinestones, seam binding and stars.

Family **by Terri Davenport**

Terri Davenport's holiday tree receives a colorful, sentimental touch and yours can, too, when photos and scrapbooking supplies meet plain ornaments and alterable objects.

How To:

To create a star, purchase an ornament and cover with walnut ink. Use the ornament as a template to trim the patterned paper. Adhere the paper to the ornament, then back the photo with cardstock and patterned paper. Add rub-ons and attach to the ornament. To create a block, wrap a toy block as if it were a present. Add an eyescrew to the top and tie a bow before adding the photo.

Terri's Tip:

Throw an ornament-making party for both seasoned crafters and non-scrapbookers. You'll have fun, and help will be on hand for those who need it!

Supplies *Textured cardstock:* Prism Papers; *Patterned paper and decorative tape:* Chloe's Closet, Imagination Project; *Rub-ons:* Chloe's Closet and Gin-X, Imagination Project; *Ribbon:* May Arts and unknown; *Walnut ink:* Fiber Scraps; *Other:* Frame, star ornament, toy block and eyescrew.

Ornaments **by Jamie Harper**

Here's a great use for those too-small patterned-paper scraps: place them inside clear glass ornaments to give your tree a festive, homespun look. Jamie Harper hangs hers with lengths of fabric to add even more charm.

How To:

Cut various lengths and widths of patterned paper. Roll strips into coils and drop into clear ornaments. Use a skewer to guide the strips. Hang the ornaments with fabric strips.

Jamie's Tip:

Make sure to use double-sided patterned paper for the most colorful results.

Supplies *Patterned papers:* Carolee's Creations; *Ornaments and fabric:* Jo-Ann Stores.

Family Forever by Darcee Waddoups

Tame the piles of paper, bills, forms and reminders in your home with an organizer that's as decorative as it is functional. Darcee Waddoups designed a gorgeous system, which could also be used to store scrapbook supplies, a child's school work or office supplies.

How To:

Purchase a filing system. Cover with patterned paper and embellishments. Decorate notebooks, folders and more to fit inside the organizer.

Darcee's Tip:

To simplify the project, fill the organizer with plain file folders and use premade embellishments.

Supplies *Organizer:* Rubbermaid; *Patterned papers:* Rusty Pickle, Making Memories and K&Company; *Rub-ons:* K&Company; *Charms:* Nunn Design; *Texture template, embossing tool and paper clips:* Carolee's Creations; *Buttons:* Making Memories; *Acrylic paint:* Delta Technical Coatings; *Embossing powder:* Stampendous!; *Stamping ink:* Making Memories, Ink It! and Ranger Industries; *Brads:* Lasting Impressions for Paper; *Leafing pen:* Krylon; *Other:* File folders, small clipboard, notebook and thread.

Ornaments by Christy Tomlinson

Every year, each member of Christy Tomlinson's family adds a new ornament to their Christmas tree. Consider adding pieces like these to your Christmas tree. Not only do they bring a little sparkle, they're also a great way to show off beloved photos from the past year.

How To:

To create the hat-pin ornament, print a photo to fit inside a metal tag and adhere. Poke the pin through the tag and replace the pin's cover. Add ribbon as an accent and to hang the ornament. To create the block ornament, drill a hole through the center of a plain block and paint. Thread wire through the hole, add beads and ribbon, then twist off the ends. Add photos and hang with ribbon.

Christy's Tip:

Save time by using a pre-beaded hat pin. If you want to make your own, however, simply use a corsage pin and add a small piece of cork as the stopper at the bottom.

SQUARE ORNAMENT
Supplies *Ribbon:* American Crafts and C.M. Offray & Son; *Metal snowflake accent and acrylic paint:* Making Memories; *Computer fonts:* CK Chemistry and CK Elegant, "Fresh Fonts" CD, *Creating Keepsakes; Other:* Craft wire, beads and wood block.

ROUND ORNAMENT
Supplies *Ribbon:* Making Memories, May Arts and C.M. Offray & Son; *Metal tag:* Making Memories; *Rub-ons:* Chatterbox; *Other:* Hat pin.

Painter's Palette
by Danielle Donaldson

Add interest to your walls with a colorful piece like the one created by Danielle Donaldson. Covered with photos and accents, the altered painter's palette serves as home decor and as an inspiration piece— each space represents a different design technique in balance, form, color or texture.

How To:

Lightly sand a plastic painter's palette before coating with paint or another medium. Add photos and embellishments to the receptacles with strong adhesive.

Danielle's Tip:

Small decorative pieces are the perfect way to experiment with new mediums, combine new colors or try new techniques.

Supplies *Patterned papers:* KI Memories and Chatterbox; *Metal accents:* Making Memories and Accent Depot; *Fabric tag:* me & my BIG ideas; *Ribbon:* May Arts and Artistic Expressions; *Label tape:* Dymo; *Letter stickers:* BasicGrey and American Crafts; *Rub-ons:* Making Memories; *Plastic monogram:* Deluxe Designs; *Stamping ink:* Ranger Industries; *Pens:* Stampin' Up! and EK Success; *Other:* Palette, flowers, slide mount, buttons and cork.

Fabulous Finds
by Heather Jones

Everyday household items hold limitless possibilities when paired with a little creative license. For example, a basic lamp shade can be instantly transformed with some fashionable handmade paper, beads, sequins or other embellishments. Look around your home, salvage yards, garage sales and consignment stores for items that can easily be altered with just a few simple supplies.

- Decorate an empty tin paint can (you can purchase clean, unused cans at craft stores) with scrapbook supplies and use it as a family time capsule.
- Search for old books at flea markets and garage sales and decoupage or refinish the cover and interior pages. You can also hollow out an area inside the book, creating a space to hold trinkets or jewelry.
- Old cigar boxes can easily be transformed into note, jewelry or treasure boxes for your kids and are fun and easy to decorate.
- Use an old license plate cut in half as the cover for a journal or scrapbook.
- Keep your eye out for cool tin, ceramic or glass containers that can be used to hold supplies in your craft room.
- Use an old map as patterned paper for scrapbook projects.
- Cut images from brochures, magazines and postcards and insert them inside metal disks or metal-rimmed tags. Attach a magnet to the back and use them as retro refrigerator magnets.
- Decoupage an ordinary frame with photocopied picture images, bits of tissue paper, magazine cutouts, ribbon and other items.

Photo Clock **by Renee Villalobos Campa**

If you're not a "clock watcher" now, you will be after creating a photo clock like the one designed by Renee Villalobos Campa. An adorable photo and colorful embellishments will give you a dose of inspiration and a sentimental look back whenever you check the time.

How To:
Disassemble a clock and remove the numbers from its face. Use the clock face as a template to trim your photos and patterned paper. Adhere photos, paper, ribbon and numbers with strong tape. Reassemble the clock.

Renee's Tip:
When purchasing a clock to alter, find one with enough space between the hands and face to allow you to add bulky embellishments without interfering with the function of the clock.

Supplies *Patterned paper, double-sided tape and hole punch:* Provo Craft; *Ribbon:* Making Memories, *Other:* Clock.

Memories in the Making **by Denise Pauley**

Do you need a "do not disturb" sign to preserve your precious "me time"? A door sign like the one by Denise Pauley is ideal for letting the family know you're in scrapping mode. Design hangers for every room in the house and include such messages as "Shh ... baby is asleep," "homework in progress" or "Dad's day off."

How To:
Paint a wood door hanger with acrylic paint and sand lightly. Trim photos and attach with double-stick tape. Embellish with stamped shapes, rub-ons, ribbon and charms.

Denise's Tip:
Add texture to the background by painting with a light color and allowing it to dry before covering it with a darker shade. Once dry, sand the edges and surface lightly until the lighter color shows through in spots.

Supplies *Letter and shape rubber stamps:* Fontwerks; *Rub-on letters:* KI Memories; *Rub-on shapes:* MOD, Autumn Leaves; *Epoxy letters:* Making Memories; *Stamping ink:* StazOn, Tsukineko; *Acrylic paint:* Delta Technical Coatings and Plaid Enterprises; *Ribbon:* Maya Road; *Charms:* Two Peas in a Bucket; *Jump rings:* Darice; *Other:* Wood door hanger.

Cherish by Janet Hopkins

Place an inspirational quote where you'll see it several times a day: on the face of a previously plain wall clock. Janet Hopkins hung one, adorned with rub-ons, as a constant reminder to cherish the day.

How To:
Spray-paint the frame of a clock to suit your decor. Use rub-ons to add a poignant quote to the clock face. Add rhinestones to the hands for sparkle.

Janet's Tip:
To pre-plan your design and make sure all the words will fit, print the quote in a font size that matches the rub-ons you plan to use. Place it over the clock face to determine where each line of the quote should start.

Supplies *Clock:* Ikea; *Rub-ons:* Making Memories, The Beary Patch and Heidi Swapp for Advantus; *Rhinestones:* Heidi Swapp for Advantus; *Spray paint:* Jo-Ann Stores.

Anderson Family by Wendy Sue Anderson

When Wendy Sue Anderson needed a board to hang in the kitchen to save notes, memos and reminders, she didn't settle for an ordinary corkboard. Instead, a magnet board adorned with photos and accents is not only functional, but also decorative and filled with family memories.

How To:
Purchase a premade magnet board. Paint the frame, lightly sand it and then rub with furniture scratch cover. Embellish with rub-ons, photos and accents. Add pins and brads for additional accents. Hang a mini frame from a drawer pull.

Wendy Sue's Tips:
Don't worry about making everything perfect. Use photos you love and you'll enjoy the board, no matter what. Using removable adhesive will also allow you to change the photos often.

Supplies *Magnet board:* Provo Craft; *Acrylic paint, rub-on letters, stick pins, brads, metal frame and accents:* Making Memories; *Ribbon:* Making Memories and unknown; *Drawer pull:* The Home Depot; *Other:* Antiquing medium and Old English Scratch Cover.

ANDERSON & FAMILY

est. 1993

Memories by Shelley Anderson

Give your office a punch of color. Shelley Anderson wanted a board that would spruce up her scrap space and help gather cards, photos and tidbits. Her design fits the bill by combining bright patterned papers and floral accents with a magnet board that allows her to update items easily.

How To:

Cover the outside of a magnet board with patterned paper and decorative tape. Add photos, embellishments and memorabilia to the front of the board. Hang with fabric strips.

Shelley's Tip:

To create a color-coordinated board and simplify the design process, choose papers and embellishments from the same company and line.

Supplies *Patterned papers, decorative tape and fabric strips:* Gin-X, Imagination Project; *Frame, flower clock and clip:* MSC Industries; *Magnetic storage container:* Michaels; *Silver clip:* Ikea; *Silk flowers:* Crafts Direct; *Other:* Brown magnet and buttons.

Create a Work of Art by Vanessa Reyes

Is your child an artist in training? Vanessa Reyes's daughter has created so many little masterpieces, she needed a clever way to exhibit the artwork. A revamped shadow box gave Vanessa the perfect space to showcase some of the pieces along with a photo of the young designer.

How To:

Add a photo and accents to the box. Have your child draw pictures on white cardstock and adhere them to an accordion-fold book. Cut colored pencils to size and add them, along with other embellishments.

Vanessa's Tip:

Create a similar display to showcase special projects or photos that celebrate a holiday or season.

Supplies *Patterned papers:* American Crafts, Autumn Leaves and Scrapworks; *Textured cardstock:* Bazzill Basics Paper; *Chipboard letters, plastic letters and acetate letters:* Heidi Swapp for Advantus; *Metal word and crystal brad:* Making Memories; *Letter brads:* Paper Studio; *Chipboard flowers:* Maya Road; *Metal-rimmed tag:* Colorbök; *Ribbon:* Autumn Leaves and May Arts; *Number stickers:* Heidi Grace Designs; *Letter stamps:* Hero Arts and PSX Design; *Stamping ink:* StazOn, Tsukineko; *Other:* Shadow box and colored pencils.

137

Butterfly Surprise by Teresa McFayden

A simple shadow box makes a big impact with a 3-D butterfly adorning a whimsical photo. This image hangs in Teresa McFayden's hallway and never fails to generate a smile.

How To:

Print the photo to fit inside a cigar box. Remove the box lid with a craft knife. Punch butterflies from patterned paper and adhere them in a stack to the nose on the photo. Embellish the box with twill and buttons. Hang the box with lengths of twill.

Teresa's Tip:

Using adhesive dots to mount the twill makes the project a snap to complete.

Supplies *Patterned papers, printed twill and buttons:* foof-a-La, Autumn Leaves; *Butterfly punch:* EK Success; *Other:* Cigar box.

Happy by Stacy McFadden

Why pay a premium for a print to hang on your wall? Get the shade, style and subject you like by designing your own decor. Stacy McFadden used computer fonts as a template for the colorful, hand-cut letters that make up the touching Mother Teresa quote.

How To:

Select a quote. Design the text in a photo-editing program and print it in reverse on the backside of a sheet of cardstock. Trim the letters with a craft knife, then arrange and adhere them to the background. Insert the piece in a frame and hang.

Stacy's Tip:

If you'd prefer not to use a craft knife, use die-cut, punched or pre-cut letters for the quote instead.

Supplies *Textured cardstock:* Prism Papers; *Quote:* Mother Teresa; *Heart punches:* Emagination Crafts.

Let NO ONE ever COME TO YOU without leaving happier

SW

It is my firm belief that we are all artists, but do you believe the same about yourself? It took me a while to come to this realization myself, but once I did, I felt free. There are no rules in art, so there were no more rules for me for scrapping.

You may not agree with me when I say you are an artist, but you will have to become one in order to complete your assignment.

I said above that there are no rules in art, but this is my book, so I will give you one: When you create your page, you will call yourself an artist. You will call yourself an artist, the place you work your studio the supplies you use your medium, and your completed page your work.

That's it. There are no other limitations. Topic, colors and supplies you use are your own. Your creative potential has just been laid completely open- how does that feel?

Once you are done, title your work and place your information on the back. Please also include a few words about your experience. How do you feel when I call you an artist? Did you like having no limitations? And most importantly, has this changed anything for you?

Art **by April Peterson**

After giving members of her circle-journal group swatches of canvas on which to complete their projects about "the artist within," April Peterson knew the results would give a great motivational touch to her scraproom wall. The piece is a colorful, textural and evocative look at artists at play.

How To:
Send 5" x 7" canvases to a group of several friends and ask them to decorate them to fit a pre-determined theme. Once returned, arrange the pieces of artwork and hang as instant inspiration.

April's Tip:
Have fun when creating your canvas. There are no rules in art; if you call yourself an artist, you are one!

CANVAS #1 by Kim Mattina
Supplies *Canvas:* Fredrix; *Tissue paper:* 7gypsies; *Rubber stamps:* All Night Media (compass), Postmodern Design (ruler), Hero Arts (flower); *Acrylic paint:* Reeves; *Stamping ink:* StazOn, Tsukineko.

CANVAS #2 by Heather Uppencamp
Supplies *Canvas:* Fredrix; *Rubber stamps, flower and fastener:* Making Memories; *Acrylic paint:* Delta Technical Coatings; *Photo corners:* Provo Craft; *Other:* Tissue paper.

CANVAS #3 by Kelly Goree
Supplies *Canvas:* Fredrix; *Letter stickers:* Chatterbox; *Acrylic paint, matte medium and spray paint:* Plaid Enterprises; *Decoupage medium:* Mod Podge, Plaid Enterprises; *Rub-ons:* Scrapworks (floral), The C-Thru Ruler Co. ("Love" phrase); *Mask:* Heidi Swapp for Advantus; *Pen:* Zig Millennium, EK Success.

CANVAS #4 by Carol Banks
Supplies *Canvas:* Fredrix; *Patterned paper:* BasicGrey; *Foam stamps and page pebbles:* Making Memories; *Acrylic paint:* Plaid Enterprises; *Decoupage medium:* Mod Podge, Plaid Enterprises; *Ribbon:* May Arts; *Letter stickers:* Nostalgiques, EK Success; *Button:* Junkitz; *Circle punch:* Family Treasures; *Computer font:* Black Adder, ITC.

CANVAS #5 by Jessie Baldwin
Supplies *Canvas:* Fredrix; *Acrylic paint:* Plaid Enterprises; *Pen:* Sharpie, Sanford.

CANVAS #6 by Amber Baley
Supplies *Canvas:* Fredrix; *Textured cardstock:* Bazzill Basics Paper; *Patterned papers:* My Mind's Eye and BasicGrey; *Dimensional adhesive:* Diamond Glaze, JudiKins; *Molding paste:* Golden; *Acrylic paint:* Delta Technical Coatings; *Computer fonts:* AL Uncle Charles, "Essential Fonts" CD, Autumn Leaves; Jane Austen, downloaded from the Internet; *Other:* Thread and jute.

CANVAS #7 by Sherry Laffoon
Supplies *Canvas:* Fredrix; *Patterned paper:* Christina Cole for Provo Craft; *Stickers:* Mustard Moon; *Rub-ons:* BasicGrey and Making Memories; *Ribbon:* C.M. Offray & Son; *Flower:* Michaels; *Dimensional adhesive:* Diamond Glaze, JudiKins; *Acrylic paint:* Jacquard Products and Making Memories; *Gold powder:* Jacquard Products; *Other:* Tissue paper.

CANVAS #8 by Melissa Ackerman
Supplies *Canvas:* Fredrix; *Rub-ons:* Making Memories ("Color," "Mystery" and "Art"), The C-Thru Ruler Co. ("Freedom" and "Imagination"); *Die cuts:* QuicKutz; *Acrylic paint and varnish:* Delta Technical Coatings; *Paint pen:* Krylon.

CANVAS #9 by Jen Nichols
Supplies *Canvas:* Fredrix; *Patterned papers:* Mustard Moon and Daisy Hill; *Mulberry paper:* Provo Craft; *Acrylic paint:* Plaid Enterprises; *Charm:* Darice; *Vintage image and mini crystal beads:* DiBona Designs; *Decoupage medium:* Mod Podge, Plaid Enterprises; *Embossing powder:* Ranger Industries; *Page pebbles:* Jo-Ann Scrap Essentials; *Corsage pin:* Atlantic; *Pen:* Zig Writer, EK Success; *Other:* Ribbon.

CANVAS #10 by April Peterson
Supplies *Canvas:* Fredrix; *Acrylic paint:* Plaid Enterprises; *Decoupage medium:* Mod Podge, Plaid Enterprises; *Letter stickers:* Mustard Moon; *Computer font:* AL Uncle Charles, "Essential Fonts" CD, Autumn Leaves; *Other:* Tissue paper.

Cub's Fan **by Joy Uzarraga**

Show your allegiance to a sports team with a cute shadow box like the one created by Joy Uzarraga. A piece combining photos of the sports fan, arena or stadium along with ticket stubs, quotes from announcers, themed stickers and other memorabilia makes a fun addition to a game room or office wall.

How To:
Create a quote using rub-ons. Embellish a photo mat with dimensional stickers before adhering the photo to the back.

Joy's Tip:
Keep it simple to keep the focus on the photos. Themed, dimensional stickers are the perfect touches for a fast and easy keepsake.

Supplies *Shadow box:* Target; *Dimensional stickers:* Jolee's Boutique, Sticko for EK Success; *Rub-ons:* 7gypsies.

Pool Time **by Shelley Anderson**

Brighten your patio table with a serving tray adorned with vivid embellishments. Shelley Anderson decorated one—which would also make great seasonal decor for a kitchen or scraproom wall—with a summery picture and dimensional flowers, tags and accents.

How To:

Paint an unfinished serving tray with acrylic paints. Attach flowers, photos and embellishments with decoupage medium. Add fabrics to the handles as a finishing touch.

Shelley's Tip:

Be sure to use thin coats of adhesive when adhering elements to the tray to prevent warping.

Supplies *Patterned papers, rub-ons, tags and decorative tape:* Gin-X, Imagination Project; *Silk flowers and wood goggles:* Michaels; *"Fun" sticker:* Creative Imaginations; *Binder clips:* Target; *Acrylic paint:* Making Memories.

Kenzie **by Kate Teague**

This set of coasters by Kate Teague is a cute and cool addition to any coffee table. The functional coasters can be used or simply displayed. Consider creating a set to represent each holiday, season or special occasion.

How To:

Create images on the computer with digital papers and elements. Print the images onto transfer paper. Follow manufacturer instructions to transfer the images to the tiles. Wash off the transfer paper and seal.

Kate's Tip:

Stick with a simple design and use a similar element—such as a monogram—on each coaster for unity.

Supplies *Digital papers, cardboard letter, file folder, photo corners and date stamp:* Katie Pertiet, downloaded from *www.designerdigitals.com*; *Tile transfer kit:* Tilano Fresco, downloaded from *www.tilanofresco.com*; *Floral brush:* Maryann Wise; *File tab:* Kellie Mize, downloaded from *www.designerdigitals.com*.

WWW.CREATINGKEEPSAKES.COM

A by Shelley Anderson

Clipboards are an ideal canvas, sturdy enough to withstand a host of altering techniques. Shelley Anderson layered hers with paper, quotes, ribbon and other accents to frame a photo of her daughter. Though decorated clipboards can still be functional, Shelley plans to keep this on her wall.

How To:

Cover a clipboard with patterned paper. Add a photo and embellishments, such as definitions, ribbon and fabric strips.

Shelley's Tip:

Give your project an antique look by sanding and distressing the cardstock and patterned paper before adhering it to the clipboard.

Supplies *Patterned papers, textured cardstock, stickers, tacks and photo corners:* Chatterbox; *Photo turns:* 7gypsies; *Flower, wooden "A" and fabric strips:* Michaels; *Acrylic paint:* Making Memories; *Chipboard:* Office Depot; *Stamping ink:* StazOn, Tsukineko; *Ribbon:* C.M. Offray & Son.

Lessons in Living by Michaela Young-Mitchell

With blank clipboards as a foundation, Michaela Young-Mitchell designed these eye-catching projects that show off photos of her children. With cool "life lessons" stamped on tags and tucked into pockets, the pieces are not only decorative, but inspirational, too.

How To:

Coat clipboards with gesso, then add ink or paint as desired. Add photos and embellish with ribbon, charms and flowers. Journal on the tags, then decorate and adhere inside the bags.

Michaela's Tip:

These altered clipboards also make great gifts—choose colors to match the recipient's decorating scheme and use themed quotes paired with appropriate photos.

Supplies *Clipboards:* Wal-Mart; *Textured cardstock:* Prism Papers; *Lacing brads, thumbtack brads and "Family" charm:* SnapStamps; *Copper word, antique copper brad, ribbon and word ribbons:* Making Memories; *Ribbon:* Wrights, C.M. Offray & Son, Maya Road, May Arts and Doodlebug Design; *Letter stamps:* PSX Design; *Stamping ink:* ColorBox, Clearsnap; *Paper flowers:* Prima and Making Memories; *Letter template:* QuicKutz; *Shipping tags:* Avery; *Gesso:* Liquitex; *Bag and tag:* Paperbilities; *Pen:* Zig Writer, EK Success.

Photo Boxes **by Candace Leonard**

Kick a stack of plain photo boxes up a notch with decoupage medium or acrylic paint. Take a cue from Candace Leonard and tailor your containers to suit their contents—check out the flames on the box of Hot Wheels and the bold floral motif covering the box of Hawaii photos.

How To:

Cover photo boxes with acrylic paint (use masks to create a pattern), rub-ons or patterned paper. Add a label to the front to identify the contents.

Candace's Tip:

Don't have time to wait for paint or decoupage medium to dry? For a quicker box, simply stamp images onto it or add rub-ons for a quick makeover.

Supplies *Patterned paper:* KI Memories; *Rub-ons:* Making Memories and KI Memories; *Masks:* Heidi Swapp for Advantus; *Acrylic paint:* Krylon; *Computer fonts:* 2Peas Jack Frost and AL Worn Machine, downloaded from *www.two-peasinabucket.com*; Hootie, downloaded from the Internet.

Decoupage
by Heather Jones

Derived from a French word meaning "to cut up or out," decoupage involves creating a collage look using scraps, ephemera and memorabilia. Loaded with customization options, this technique offers you the flexibility to pack your personality in to your project. Not only is it easy and fun, but you'll find this is the perfect project to use leftover scraps and small memorabilia. Scrapbook tags and accents, funky fridge magnets and unique photo boxes are just a few of the projects you can create with decoupage.

Basic Decoupage Steps:

❶ Collect your favorite quotes, magazine cutouts, patterned-paper scraps, ticket stubs, old stamps and more, and cut or tear the items into the desired sizes. For a more random look, use many different sizes and alternate between using a clean cut and tearing.

❷ Arrange the items on the selected surface area in a collage pattern, using adhesive or decoupage medium to adhere the pieces.

❸ Smooth out remaining wrinkles with a brayer or burnisher.

❹ Brush the entire surface with glossy or matte decoupage medium or glaze using a foam brush. Allow to dry completely.

Consider these ideas for a decoupage project:

An old suitcase as a storage trunk for craft supplies
Picture frames
Lampshades
The cover and interior pages of old books
Your workstation or desk
The front of a photo album
Storage and photo boxes
Glass jars

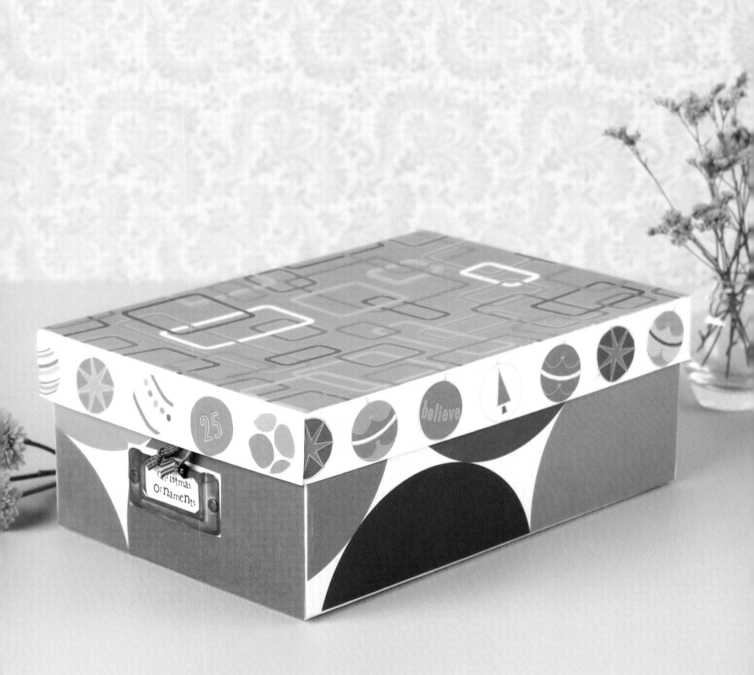

WWW.CREATINGKEEPSAKES.COM

CREATING KEEPSA

Photo Boxes **by Tarri Botwinski**

Tarri Botwinski is the hit of the scrapbooking party when she pulls up with these decorated boxes. Covered with patterned paper, stickers and other accents, the previously unfinished wood boxes are now adorable storage containers for photos and other scrapbooking tools.

How To:
Use decoupage medium to adhere patterned paper, ribbon and cardstock to unfinished boxes. Add letter stickers and a silk flower, then coat again with medium to seal. Drill holes in the top of the smaller box to insert rivets that will hold a ribbon handle.

Tarri's Tip:
Be sure to let the project dry completely before adding the top coat. If the box is still wet, the paper may wrinkle or tear. Also, be sure to let the top coat dry completely before closing the box to prevent sticking.

Supplies *Patterned papers, textured cardstock, die cuts, letter stickers, rivets and photo corners:* Chatterbox; *Ribbon:* C.M. Offray & Son; *Decoupage medium:* Mod Podge, Plaid Enterprises; *Other:* Boxes, stain and silk flower.

Milestones **by Nicole Keller**

Do you have a milestone you want to commemorate? Moving to Texas was such an important highlight for Nicole Keller's family, she wanted to honor it with a striking piece of decor. She used various paints and glazes to revamp a decorated wood box that now houses mini albums that document the family move.

How To:
Sand the box to remove any existing design. Paint the box, then sand and "age" it with antiquing glaze. Fill the box with mini albums featuring special photos, clip art, stamped images and stickers.

Nicole's Tip:
There's no way to mess up when you're aging a project. Paint and sand away until you get the amount of distressing you desire.

Supplies *Box:* Hobby Lobby; *Letter stamps:* Hero Arts; *Acrylic paint:* Plaid Enterprises; *Small and mini album die cuts:* Sizzix, Provo Craft; *Stickers:* Jolee's Boutique, Sticko for EK Success; *Twill:* Maya Road; *Antiquing glaze:* Delta Technical Coatings; *Dimensional adhesive:* Diamond Glaze, JudiKins; *Computer fonts:* Carbonated Gothic, downloaded from the Internet; 2Peas Billboard, downloaded from *www.twopeasinabucket.com*; *Other:* Sandpaper and stamping ink.

149

keepsakes 4

Heirlooms aren't just keepsakes to be inherited, they're also treasures you can create. They might record family milestones, showcase your hobbies and holiday celebrations, or reveal the bonds you share with close friends. Wouldn't you love such a glimpse at your ancestors' lives? Think of the joy someone will feel years from now upon discovering an item you created today. Let the wealth of projects in this chapter start you on the road to designing something that your family will pass down from generation to generation.

Isabelle by April Peterson

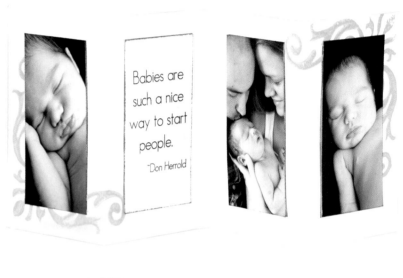

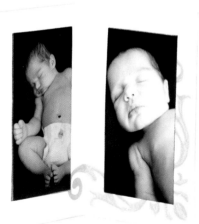

Imagine designing a gorgeous baby announcement with supplies you have on hand. With acrylic paint, a transparency and a few accents, April Peterson created an ethereal and adorable showcase for several striking photos and pertinent facts.

How To:

Cut an 8½" x 11" transparency in half, length-wise. Stamp a design with acrylic paint and allow to dry. Fold the piece in half and in half again. Print six photos and trim to 1¾" x 3¼". Adhere the photos to line up completely when folded. Print the quote, trim to the same size as the photos and adhere. Attach ribbon to close.

April's Tip:

If you're making several of these announcements, save time by creating them assembly-line style—cut all the transparencies first, then stamp, then add photos, etc.

Supplies *Textured cardstock:* Bazzill Basics Paper; *Ribbon:* May Arts and C.M. Offray & Son; *Transparency:* Staples; *Foam stamps and acrylic paint:* Making Memories; *Computer font:* Maximo, downloaded from the Internet; *Other:* Button and clasp.

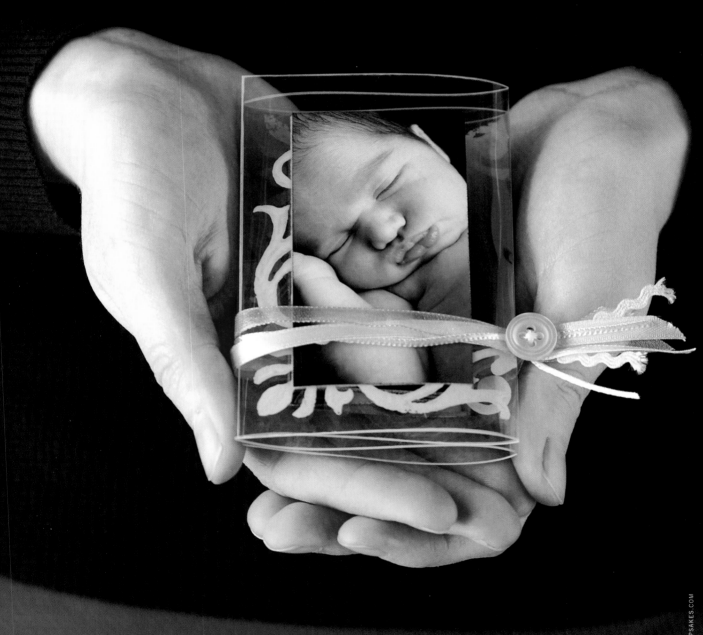

We have been
blessed
with a tiny new
daughter .

Lily Grace
June 9, 1999
7 pounds 1 ounce
19 inches

love   joy

baby

SWEET

Sweet as sugar,
as good as gold,
our precious
baby girl,
a miracle
to behold!

BABY GIRL

BABY GIRL
A LITTLE BIT OF HEAVEN   precious
precious

Lily Grace **by Kristi Barnes**

Turn a baby announcement into cherished decor by mounting it on canvas along with pretty baby-themed embellishments. Kristi Barnes designed a piece featuring her daughter's announcement, which hangs as a memento alongside her daughter's blessing gown.

How To:
Purchase an 8" x 8" canvas. Cover the canvas with patterned papers and add baby's birth announcement. Adorn with ribbon and baby-themed accents.

Kristi's Tip:
Be sure to adhere everything securely to prevent items from falling off once the piece is hung. Consider using double-stick tape, decoupage medium or adhesive dots for particularly heavy items.

Supplies *Patterned papers and metal embellishment:* Making Memories; *Page coaster:* Cloud 9 Design; *Ribbon:* May Arts; *Stamping ink:* ColorBox, Clearsnap; *Other:* Canvas.

Grow **by Jennifer Gallacher**

Rather than mark on the wall, keep a permanent record of your child's growth with a chart that can be updated and treasured through the years. Whimsical phrases and colorful brad bars make Jennifer Gallacher's project as sweet as it is significant.

How To:
Cut three widths of 12" x 12" paper and stitch together to form one long strip. Add circles in varying sizes and rub-on phrases. Add brad bars to denote measurements.

Jennifer's Tip:
If you use brad bars as height markers, be sure to measure and mark the locations before piercing the paper.

Supplies *Patterned papers:* The C-Thru Ruler Co. and Karen Foster Design; *Ribbon, foam stamps and epoxy letters:* Li'l Davis Designs; *Acrylic paint and square eyelets:* Making Memories; *Brad bars:* Karen Foster Design; *Rub-on phrase:* Déjà Views, The C-Thru Ruler Co.; *Circle punches:* McGill.

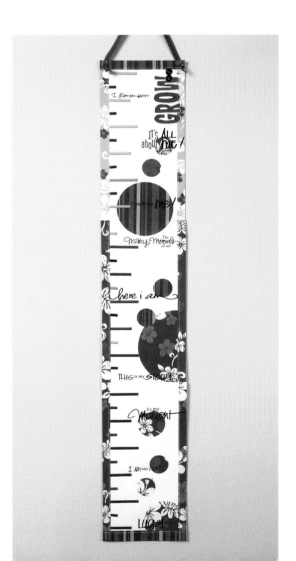

Sassy by Janet Hopkins

Does your child have a favorite item of clothing? Once outgrown, don't dispose of it, display it! Janet Hopkins created a pretty shadow box to showcase her daughter's beloved dress, which, sadly, no longer fits. The project allows her to remember the dress because it's now a lovely piece of art in her room.

How To:

Purchase a shadow box frame and spray-paint it light green. Add coordinating photos and accessories to the interior. Place the dress over the frame board and wrap the remaining portions behind to tuck into the frame.

Janet's Tip:

When choosing a shadow box, consider the size of the item of clothing you plan to place inside. Even light-weight items can be bulky when folded over.

Supplies *Shadow box:* Hobby Lobby; *Fuzzy rub-ons and flower rhinestones:* Heidi Swapp for Advantus; *Spray paint:* Jo-Ann Stores; *Label:* Making Memories; *Pink clip:* Design Originals; *Pink envelope and wood frame:* Li'l Davis Designs; *Computer font:* Quick Wit by Tia Bennett, downloaded from *www.two-peasinabucket.com*; *Other:* Tag.

Heirloom Handiwork by Allison Kimball

Allison Kimball turns artwork into heirloom with some homespun sewn edges and simple ornamental touches. Unadorned black frames make the perfect home for the pieces, which can become treasured artwork or appreciated gifts for grandparents or teachers.

How To:

Lace piece: Trim black cardstock for your background and use a few stitches to hold the lace in place. Add a quote to the glass with rub-ons.

Artwork: Trace your child's artwork onto fabric with a thin black marker. Dry-brush acrylic paint onto the image. Stitch around the marker lines with embroidery floss. Mat with chipboard and frame.

Allison's Tip:

You can use any artwork to create heirloom pieces—have your child draw a different picture for every season!

Supplies *Textured cardstock:* Prism Papers; *Rub-ons:* KI Memories and Doodlebug Design; *Acrylic paint:* Delta Technical Coatings; *Pens:* American Crafts and Sigma; *Embroidery floss:* DMC; *Other:* Frames and muslin.

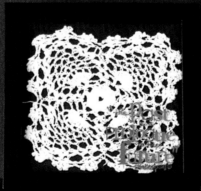

| WWW.CREATINGKEEPSAKES.COM

Cherish by Irma Gabbard

With a photo purse like the one fashioned by Irma Gabbard, you can now add an item to the mental checklist as you leave the door—keys, wallet, makeup … memories? Designed with durable fabric, the tote keeps all of your necessities organized and shows off recent photos.

How To:

Purchase the purse pattern along with fabric and a clear plastic tablecloth. Cut out the pattern and arrange ribbon, rickrack and plastic on one side of the pattern. Attach with machine-stitching, leaving an opening on top to add photos. Sew the purse according to instructions. Add paint and embossing enamel to metal words and attach to the purse.

Irma's Tip:

If you don't sew, you can start with a premade purse and use fusible stitching tape and an iron to attach trims.

Supplies *Purse pattern:* Amy Butter; *Ribbon:* May Arts; *Fabric:* Waverly; *Metal words:* Making Memories; *Word charm:* Pebbles Inc.; *Acrylic paint:* Delta Technical Coatings; *Rickrack:* C.M. Offray & Son; *Other:* Vintage black trim.

Duet by Sande Krieger

Capture a complete memory with sound as well as sight. Sande Krieger preserved this moment of her sons playing a duet by placing photos and written details on a layout and an audio recording nearby. Think of what memories you can enhance by keeping something you can listen to as well.

How To:

Design a scrapbook page showing children playing a duet on the piano. Record the music on a flat recording device and store with the layout.

Sande's Tip:

If you're just starting out scrapbooking, don't worry about the design. The most important thing is to write down your thoughts, add photos and, if you can, make a recording to go with it on a CD or tape.

Supplies *Patterned papers:* KI Memories; *Textured cardstock:* Prism Papers and Provo Craft; *Letter stamps:* Technique Tuesday; *Stamping ink:* Ranger Industries; *Rub-ons:* Scenic Route Paper Co.; *Digital recorder:* Sound Stripes; *"x2" and epoxy square flower:* Christina Cole for Provo Craft; *Pen:* Zig Millennium, EK Success; *Computer font:* AL Remington, downloaded from *www.twopeasinabucket.com.*

Our Year in Review *by Lana Rickabaugh*

Even the most diligent scrapbookers end up with piles of spare photos. Lana Rickabaugh rescued hers from a box under the bed and placed them in a container where they can be organized, protected and—most of all—seen. The box invites family and friends to view the photos, while labeled folders ensure they're returned to the proper spot.

How To:

Sand the box and paint the frames and knob. Attach patterned papers to the surfaces with decoupage medium. Sand the rough edges and add paint to distress. Add text to photos with photo-editing software and size to fit within the frames. Trim the file folders to fit inside the box and stamp event titles on the tabs.

Lana's Tip:

This project is a great way to use leftover supplies by using scraps of cardstock and paper to create the file folders and embellishments.

Supplies *Wooden box:* Jo-Ann Stores; *Patterned papers:* Carolee's Creations, Design Originals and Provo Craft; *Ribbon:* C.M. Offray & Son; *Letter stamps:* Hero Arts; *Foam stamps:* Making Memories; *Stickers:* Design Originals; *Stamping ink:* VersaMark, Tsukineko; *Acrylic paint:* Delta Technical Coatings.

Mary *by Carey Johnson*

To design a bit of decorative history about her mother, Carey Johnson combined her mom's childhood memories, photos and a book into a nostalgic shadow box. Carey's next piece will be a shadow box about her father that features some of his childhood toys. What types of items would you include in shadow boxes for your friends and family?

How To:

Purchase a shadow box. Adhere fabric to poster board and glue it to the back of the shadow box. Add journaling, patterned papers and accents to the fabric. Create a mini book with photos and attach with liquid adhesive.

Carey's Tip:

If possible, interview the recipient to collect interesting facts and tidbits to add to the shadow box.

Supplies *Shadow box:* Pottery Barn; *Patterned paper:* Wild Asparagus, My Mind's Eye; *Metal letters:* American Crafts; *Decoupage medium:* Mod Podge, Plaid Enterprises; *Antique book: Mrs. Wiggs of the Cabbage Patch* by Alice Caldwell Hegan, Grossup and Dunlap, New York; *Stamping ink:* StazOn, Tsukineko; *Journal jewelry:* 7gypsies; *Transparency:* OfficeMax; *Computer font:* Headache, downloaded from the Internet; *Other:* Fabric.

Born: February 12, 1947
When I grow up: Elementary Teacher
Best Subject: English/Reading
Favorite Toy: Tiny Tears Doll
Favorite Hobby: Reading Books
Item most dear: Rock-a-bye Blanket

mary

Mrs. Wiggs
of the Cabbage
Patch

BY ALICE HEGAN RICE

A Hurshweed Book

DECADES
an Opel
family history

Decades by Beth Opel

An 8½" x 11" landscape album provides the foundation for Beth Opel's comprehensive family history project. She blended photos from each decade with family milestones and historical world events.

How To:

Decorate the album cover. Scan, trim and resize photos before printing. Design a timeline of world and family events for each decade. Choose fonts, patterned papers and accents to fit the "style" of the era. Assemble pages.

Beth's Tip:

Since the pictures and timeline tell the story here, you don't need a lot of scrapbooking "expertise" to create a unique album. The key is to choose photos carefully—select images that are dear to you or that represent your family through the decades.

COVER
Supplies *Album:* SEI; *Leather label holder:* Making Memories; *Letter sticker:* Sonnets, Creative Imaginations; *Ribbon:* C.M. Offray & Son; *Metal letters:* Karen Foster Design; *Brads:* Creative Impressions; *Computer font:* Century Gothic, Microsoft Word.

1940s
Supplies *Textured cardstock:* Bazzill Basics Paper; *Patterned paper:* Polar Bear Press; *Clock embellishment:* 7gypsies; *Trim:* Jo-Ann Stores; *Computer fonts:* CAC Futura Casual and Premi, downloaded from the Internet.

1970s
Supplies *Textured cardstock:* Bazzill Basics Paper; *Patterned paper:* Reminisce; *Sequin:* Jo-Ann Stores; *Brad:* Creative Impressions; *Computer fonts:* CAC Futura Casual and Bauhaus 93, downloaded from the Internet.

2000s
Supplies *Textured cardstock:* Bazzill Basics Paper; *Patterned paper:* Colorbök; *Trim:* Making Memories; *Computer fonts:* CAC Futura Casual and Welton Urban, downloaded from the Internet.

| WWW.CREATINGKEEPSAKES.COM

Family History
by Traci Turchin

Heritage photos—particularly those with little detail surrounding them—can be intimidating to work with. But by designing card-sized scrapbook pages to store in a decorative pail, Traci Turchin discovered a way to scrapbook the photos and information she has now, with the opportunity to add more details and images as she obtains them.

How To:

Cover a pail with patterned papers, a title and accents. Design pages with photos, journaling and embellishments. Place pages in the pail.

Traci's Tip:

Try this idea at a family reunion: send inserts to each household and ask them to add a family photo and brief story. At the reunion, they can file their layout in the section representing their branch on the family tree.

Supplies *Software:* Adobe Photoshop CS, Adobe Systems; *Decorative-pail album kit:* BasicGrey; *Patterned papers:* BasicGrey, KI Memories and Autumn Leaves; *Tag and title plate:* Autumn Leaves; *Rubber stamps:* A Muse Artstamps; *Dimensional adhesive:* Diamond Glaze, JudiKins; *Computer font:* Univers, downloaded from *www.linotype.com; Other:* Ribbon.

Linking Your Family's Past and Future
by Leslie Miller

Are you interested in creating a family tree or finding out more about your ancestors? Get started by following these steps:

1. Write down everything you know. Start with yourself and work backward to your parents, grandparents, great-grandparents, etc. Be sure to note the vital information you have about them, including full names; the dates of important events in their lives, such as birth, marriage, and death; and the places these important events took place. You may also want to note any siblings they may have had, the names of their spouses and their occupations. (*Note:* For an easy way to organize the information you are gathering, use a Pedigree Chart and a Family Group Record form. These forms are used by professional genealogists and are available at the websites listed at right.)

2. Look for documents that may be in your family's possession. Useful sources include birth, marriage and death certificates; family bibles; funeral programs; obituaries; wedding announcements; family registers; and ancestral tablets. Add this information to your pedigree charts and family group records.

3. Ask your relatives for information. People often remember tidbits of information while they're sharing stories about their ancestors. Dedicate some time to listening to and documenting any stories you may hear about your ancestors.

4. Find out if someone else has located the information. Using one of the websites listed below, search for a particular ancestor. You may find information in government records or published family records, or you may find that someone else has already found the information for you.

5. Search records for information about your ancestor. Several of the websites listed below will guide you through the process of finding copies of original records, such as censuses and birth records, based on where the person lived and the time of his or her birth, marriage or death. For example, in the Research Guidance section of FamilySearch.org, you can select the place and time, and Research Guidance will provide a list of recommended actions and records to search in priority order.

Recommended Websites:

Ancestry.com   Genhomepage.com

FamilySearch.org   Genealogical.com

FamilyTree.com   RootsWeb.com

MyFamily.com

Five Generations

by Dece Gherardini

As a simple, visual way for her daughter to learn about both sides of her family, Dece Gherardini designed a project that's appealing and informative. Creative placement of paper and embellishments turn a coin folder into a logical foundation for a piece featuring spots for each member on the family tree.

How To:

Purchase a state-quarter coin folder and strip the panels from the backing. Add stitching to patterned papers, then adhere to the cover of the folder. Adhere the patterned paper to the inside of the folder and use a craft knife to cut holes. Add journaling to cardstock that will show through the openings. Add photos and embellishments.

Dece's Tip:

When using a coin folder, a little pre-planning goes a long way. Stitching accents or poking fasteners through before you adhere the cardstock, photo or paper to the coin folder will make the process much easier.

Supplies *Textured cardstock:* Bazzill Basics Paper; *Patterned papers:* Chatterbox; *Letter stickers:* Wordsworth and American Crafts; *Rub-ons and brads:* Making Memories; *Ribbon:* May Arts; *Photo corners:* Heidi Swapp for Advantus; *Pen:* Pigma Micron, Sakura; *Computer fonts:* Georgia, Brock Script, P22 Victorian and Antique Typewriter, downloaded from the Internet; Times New Roman and Arial, Microsoft Word; CK Script, "The Best of Creative Lettering" Combo CD; CK Regal, "Creative Clips & Fonts for Special Occasions" CD; CK Stenography, "Fresh Fonts" CD, *Creating Keepsakes.*

December *by Erin Lincoln*

Searching for the perfect countdown calendar for a big event? Design one that allows you to celebrate each day with a memory of friends and family. Erin Lincoln turned a coin folder into a colorful holiday keepsake with stickers, reduced photos and spare scrapbook supplies.

How To:

To create the hole covers, adhere in this order: 1½" punched magnetic sheeting, 1¾" black cardstock, then 1½" white cardstock with sticker image. Coat the back edge of the black cardstock rim with repositionable adhesive. To create the coin holder, attach ribbon with brads. Punch 1½" circles from photos. Adhere the photos in the coin openings, and adhere the dates to the corners.

Erin's Tip:

Note that the magnetic sheeting isn't what's securing the covers onto the coin openings; it's simply making them fit tightly. The repositionable adhesive on the back of the black cardstock edge is actually what keeps the pieces in place.

Supplies *Patterned paper:* Treehouse Memories; *Specialty paper:* Paper Garden; *Letter stamps:* Fontwerks; *Stickers:* Bo-Bunny Press, me & my BIG ideas and Magenta; *Brads:* American Crafts; *Coin holder:* Bazzill Basics Paper; *Rub-ons:* BasicGrey; *Hinges:* Making Memories; *Die-cut letters:* QuicKutz; *Computer font:* Georgia, downloaded from the Internet; *Other:* Sheet magnets.

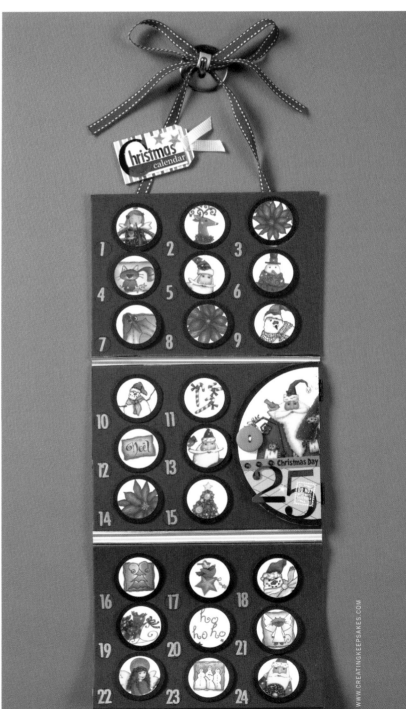

Family by Lisa Damrosch

Here's an heirloom holiday decoration
and conversation piece all in one. Lisa
Damrosch stores photos from 20 years
of family Christmas celebrations in a
decorative tin that can be added to,
passed around and discussed at family
festivities.

How To:
Decorate a pail with patterned papers, a monogram
and other accents. Create dividers with tabs.
Design a page for each year featuring a photo and
highlights. Add journaling inside the pail lid.

Lisa's Tip:
Since you're storing photos chronologically, this
idea would also work well for school portraits or
baby photos by the month.

Supplies *Decorative-pail album kit:* BasicGrey; *Tabs:* Heidi Swapp for
Advantus; *Other:* Patterned papers, ribbon, chipboard, palette and buttons.

Holidays by Teri Fode

What is it about holiday songs that instantly brings back fond family memories? Teri Fode combined the two in a keepsake album featuring sentimental song lyrics and photos of her loved ones and holiday decorations through the years.

How To:

Purchase a pre-assembled mini album. Cover a compact disc with patterned papers and use it to adorn the cover. Complete the cover and inside pages with coordinating patterned papers and embellishments, adding the song title and journaling to the right pages and photo to the left.

Teri's Tip:

Mini albums are the perfect place to use several "older" holiday photos without having to scrapbook every single image.

Supplies *Patterned papers:* Scenic Route Paper Co., Creative Imaginations and KI Memories; *Ribbon:* Making Memories, American Crafts and C.M. Offray & Son; *Photo corners:* Heidi Swapp for Advantus; *Rub-on letters:* Making Memories; *Snowflake stamp:* Duncan Enterprises; *String closures:* EK Success; *Epoxy letters:* K&Company; *Wood letters:* Paper Bliss, Westrim Crafts; *CD, staples and paper clips:* OfficeMax; *Pen:* Pigment Pro, American Crafts; *Paper flowers:* Prima; *Poinsettia:* Michaels.

the little book of holiday favorite songs

Fabric of Our Lives by Shannon Taylor

A security blanket. A worn stuffed animal. A comfy sweater. Can you remember the feel of your favorite comfort item? Shannon Taylor incorporated actual swatches of fabric to remind her family of the pieces they used to hold so dear. Leaving page protectors off the album invites readers to touch each textile.

How To:

Cover an album with quilt squares. Paint and chalk chipboard letters and wrap flowers around them. Design pages with photos, journaling, accents and textiles.

Shannon's Tip:

Don't be afraid to use textiles. You can adhere fabric in numerous ways, such as with brads, staples, double-stick tape, ribbon or stitching.

COVER
Supplies *Chipboard album and letters:* Rusty Pickle; *Rub-on letters:* Rusty Pickle and EK Success; *Quilt piece:* Created by Ginny Burks; *Paper flowers:* Prima; *Hat pin and acrylic paint:* Making Memories; *Ribbon:* Chatterbox; *Other:* Circle tag

DENIM & LEATHER PAGE
Supplies *Patterned paper:* Junkitz; *Leather paper:* K&Company; *Tags:* Rusty Pickle; *Screw brads:* Karen Foster Design; *"Explorer" metal accent:* All My Memories; *Pen:* Zig Millennium, EK Success; *Other:* Denim.

Keepsake Container by Lynne Montgomery

If you find yourself misplacing trinkets you've collected over the years, why not incorporate them into larger pieces you can treasure and display? Lynne Montgomery used unique containers and resin to seal sentimental tidbits from family vacations, trips with friends and more.

How To:

Age a tin by sanding, painting and stippling with brown ink or stamping with a quote. Trim patterned paper and adhere inside the tin. Prepare painted accents and arrange and adhere inside the tin. Mix and pour resin into the tin following manufacturer instructions.

Note: Almost any container can be filled with memorabilia. Lynne also filled a shell and a small container with memories and resin.

Lynne's Tip:

Practice working with resin before creating your final project. Test the items to see how they will react—for example, thin ribbon and paper may become transparent once the substance is poured.

BEACH
Supplies *Bookplate, word stickers, jump ring and rub-on word:* Making Memories; *Resin:* Enviro-Tex Lite; *Other:* Seashells, sand, crab leg, and rock.

LOVE TIN
Supplies *Patterned paper and cameo pin:* 7gypsies; *Metal plaque, definition stickers, acrylic paint, rub-on letters, jump rings and ribbon:* Making Memories; *Angel wings:* Darice; *Rubber stamps:* Hero Arts; *Stamping ink:* Distress Ink, Ranger Industries; *Matte medium:* Golden; *High-gloss finish:* Enviro-Finish; *Other:* Altoids tin, eye glass, key, postcard and letters cut from magazines.

GOT MILK?
Supplies *Acrylic paint, eyelet and button:* Making Memories; *Rubber stamps:* PSX Design; *Stamping ink:* StazOn, Tsukineko; *Matte medium:* Golden; *High-gloss finish:* Enviro-Finish; *Other:* Silk flowers, patterned paper, letters cut from magazine, lid from storage tin, Altoids tin and jute.

| WWW.CREATINGKEEPSAKES.COM

Our Wedding by Nicole Keller

Get your wedding memorabilia out of the closet and into a beautiful shadow box. Nicole Keller's wedding mementos remained hidden in a box since they were too bulky to fit into scrapbook albums. But with this project, they're now in a timeless display that she and her husband can enjoy.

How To:

Divide memorabilia into four piles to create a balanced composition. Open the shadow box and place the smaller items inside. Use adhesive dots to secure everything. Line the back of the shadow box with black cardstock and seal shut.

Nicole's Tip:

Shadow boxes also make great gifts for graduations, birthdays or baby showers. Create the shadow box, provide adhesives and let the recipient fill it with items of his or her choice.

Supplies *Shadow box:* Hobby Lobby; *Letter stamps:* Hero Arts; *Acrylic paint:* Plaid Enterprises; *Small and mini-album die cuts:* Sizzix, Provo Craft; *Stickers:* Jolee's Boutique, Sticko for EK Success; *Twill:* Maya Road; *Antiquing glaze:* Delta Technical Coatings; *Dimensional adhesive:* Diamond Glaze, JudiKins; *Computer fonts:* Carbonated Gothic, downloaded from the Internet; 2Peas Billboard, downloaded from *www.twopeasinabucket.com; Other:* Sandpaper and stamping ink.

2Peas Recipes by Shelley Anderson

If you've got recipes scribbled on scraps of paper, consolidate them in a container where they'll be easy to organize and store. After collecting several crock pot recipes from the online message board she frequents, Shelley Anderson placed them in a keepsake pail that can be displayed on her kitchen counter or desk.

How To:

Paint the pail with acrylic paint. Punch and adhere squares of patterned paper to the tin. Embellish the tin and decorate the card dividers before placing recipes inside.

Shelley's Tip:

Remember to sand the box before painting to help the paint adhere. To save time, purchase a pail that's already painted white, such as those typically found in craft stores.

Supplies *Decorative pail:* BasicGrey; *Textured cardstock:* Prism Papers; *Patterned paper, decorative tape and fabric strips:* Gin-X, Imagination Project; *Wood frames and tags:* Chatterbox; *Rub-ons:* Chatterbox and Gin-X, Imagination Project; *Ribbon:* Li'l Davis Designs and Chatterbox; *Stamping ink:* StazOn, Tsukineko; *Binder clips:* Target; *Acrylic paint:* Making Memories; *Buttons:* Making Memories and Michaels; *Square punch:* Creative Memories.

Their Recipes **by Leah LaMontagne**

It's time to preserve your secret family recipes. Leah LaMontagne fashioned an original project to showcase trademark recipes by the five "mother figures" in her life: her mother, her mother-in-law, her husband's grandmother and her two grand-mothers. Each tin contains a booklet with the recipe and the story surrounding it.

How To:

Format and print the recipes in a size that will fit within the circle punch. Punch recipes and photos into circles and adorn with stamped images. Laminate recipes and photos. Connect circles with pieces of bookbinding

tape, adding a circle tile in the back for durability. Punch small holes through both sides of the top photo circle and string ribbon through to tie the booklet shut. Attach a magnet to the back of each booklet.

Leah's Tip:

You don't have to confine your muffin-tin album to the kitchen. The tin is simply an innovative "frame" for booklets, pictures or other memorabilia. Try it with a variety of subjects.

Supplies *Circular tiles, scalloped tile, square tile and rubber stamps:* Technique Tuesday; *Bookbinding and acrylic paint:* Making Memories; *Stamping ink:* Tsukineko and Clearsnap; *Spray paint:* Krylon; *Rub-on:* BasicGrey; *Circle punch:* Marvy Uchida; *Photo anchors:* 7gypsies; *Mini brads:* Queen & Co.; *Computer fonts:* Bernard MT Condensed and Raavi, Microsoft Word; *Other:* Ribbon, magnets and muffin tin.

Hold a True Friend ... **by Nichol Magouirk**

A circle journal gives you the opportunity to connect and share your vision with other artists. Nichol Magouirk and friends compiled their creativity in a beautiful album that pays tribute to a mutual friend and becomes a lasting memento of their love and admiration for her.

How To:

Decorate the front and back covers of a board book. Design your entry and adhere inside the album. Send the project to other participants, asking each to design a page following the same theme.

Nichol's Tip:

When starting a circle journal, be sure to have a clear set of guidelines for everyone to follow. Try a smaller-sized album so it's not too time consuming for the participants.

COVER
Supplies *Patterned papers:* Magenta, Melissa Frances and 7gypsies; *Mini letter stickers, stickpin, buttons and ribbon:* Making Memories; *Knob, elastic and printed twill:* 7gypsies; *Rub-ons:* Li'l Davis Designs.

NICHOL'S ENTRY
Supplies *Patterned paper:* KI Memories; *Chipboard phrase, rub-ons and letter stickers:* Li'l Davis Designs; *Photo corners:* Heidi Swapp for Advantus; *Felt flowers and ribbon:* Making Memories; *Rhinestone brads:* SEI; *Rub-on monogram:* Art Warehouse, Creative Imaginations.

MELODEE'S ENTRY
Supplies *Patterned papers:* Creative Imaginations and 7gypsies; *Ribbon:* SEI; *Photo corners:* Creative Imaginations; *Brads:* American Traditional Designs and Creative Imaginations; *Sticker:* 7gypsies; *Charm lock:* The Card Connection; *Flower:* Making Memories; *Stamping ink:* ColorBox Fluid Chalk, Clearsnap.

TIPster Friends

by Susanna Tunturi-Anttila

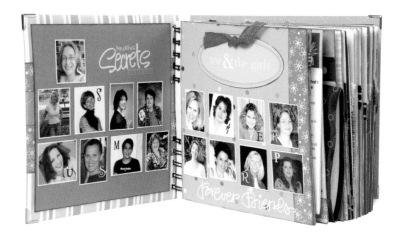

Despite the distance, bonds of online friendships may be some of the strongest you'll forge. Celebrate these relationships, as Susanna Tunturi-Anttila has, with an album that outlines the support, stories and experiences you've shared.

How To:

Gather quotes and accents that suit a particular group of friends. Adhere patterned papers and embellishments to the cover. Create pages by cutting patterned paper to size, then adding journaling and photos printed on textured cardstock. Attach an envelope and monogram to each page and include pertinent details about each friend.

Susanna's Tip:

Get everyone's input to make a more personal album; ask friends to jot down a few words or statements about one another. Create a page in back that each friend can sign in person when you get the opportunity to meet!

COVER
Supplies *Album and metal corners:* 7gypsies; *Patterned papers:* Chatterbox and KI Memories; *Stickers:* Making Memories and Creative Imaginations; *Ribbon:* May Arts and KI Memories; *Die cuts and acrylic accents:* KI Memories; *Metal word, washer and rub-on letters:* Making Memories; *"Sassy" accent:* Scrapworks; *Stamping ink:* Ranger Industries; *Wood tag:* Chatterbox; *Die cut:* Déjà Views, The C-Thru Ruler Co.; *Decoupage medium:* Mod Podge, Plaid Enterprises; *Other:* Metal chain and charm.

ME AND THE GIRLS
Supplies *Patterned papers:* Chatterbox and KI Memories; *Ribbon:* May Arts; *Rub-ons:* Déjà Views, The C-Thru Ruler Co.; *Stamping ink:* Ranger Industries; *Die cut:* Chatterbox; *Computer fonts:* 2Peas Chestnuts, downloaded from *www.twopeasinabucket.com*; P22 Garamouche, Mom's Typewriter and Hannibal Lector, downloaded from the Internet.

ADRIENNE
Supplies *Patterned papers:* KI Memories and Chatterbox; *Textured cardstock:* Bazzill Basics Paper; *Ribbon:* May Arts; *Rub-ons:* SEI; *Staples:* Making Memories; *Rub-on letters:* Chatterbox; *Stamping ink:* Ranger Industries; *Computer fonts:* 2Peas Pure Imagination, 2Peas Typo, 2Peas Airplane, 2Peas Weathered Fence, 2Peas Tasklist and 2Peas Think Small, downloaded from *www.twopeasinabucket.com*; Love Letter TW, downloaded from the Internet; *Other:* Twill, charms, thread, fabric flower and safety pin.

SUSANNA
Supplies *Patterned papers:* KI Memories and Chatterbox; *Textured cardstock:* Bazzill Basics Paper; *Ribbon:* May Arts; *Heart brads, rub-on letters, metal tag and stickers:* Making Memories; *Stamping ink:* Ranger Industries; *Tag and "Caring" sticker:* Pebbles Inc.; *Rub-on number:* SEI; *Rub-ons:* Déjà Views, The C-Thru Ruler Co.; *Computer fonts:* 2Peas Quirky, 2Peas Pure Imagination, 2Peas High Tide, 2Peas Magic Forest and AL Sandra, downloaded from *www.twopeasinabucket.com*; Love Letter TW, GF Ordner Inverted and Elvgren Pin-ups Dings, downloaded from the Internet; *Other:* Postage stamp, fabric flower and button.

girls just want to have fun

If you obey all the rules you miss all the fun.
-Katherine Hepburn

It's a girl thing.

sassy

tIpSters

quality time

epic adventures

life

Attitude is the palette
by which our lives
are painted.

girlfriends

MAY 2003

DO NOT DISTURB   NO BOYS ALLOWED

17 unique

Who's That Girl? by Shannon Taylor

Are your friends "keepers"? Shannon Taylor knows that as the years pass, she'll still cherish her closest scrapbooking friends. An interactive mini album commemorates their bond and highlights each woman's unique personality.

How To:

Cut squares and strips of patterned paper and adhere to the box. Add a title and accents. Create a page for each person, hiding the photos with interactive elements.

Shannon's Tip:

Use your imagination when creating interactive elements. Choose a product and think about different ways it can be used. Chances are you'll come up with something unique!

BOX
Supplies *Box:* Making Memories; *Patterned paper and buttons:* Junkitz; *Ribbon:* C.M. Offray & Son; *Double-sided tape:* Therm O Web.

HEATHER PRECKEL PAGE
Supplies *Patterned papers:* My Mind's Eye; *Ribbon:* C.M. Offray & Son; *Rub-on letters:* Rusty Pickle; *Paper flowers:* Prima; *Brads:* Junkitz; *Rubber stamps:* Hero Arts; *Other:* Rickrack and metal flowers.

BETHANY FIELDS PAGE
Supplies *Patterned papers:* Junkitz; *Rubber stamps:* Hero Arts; *Label tape:* Dymo; *Fabric:* The Robin's Nest; *Charms:* The Card Connection.

HOLLY VANDYNE PAGE
Supplies *Ribbon:* American Crafts; *Label tape:* Dymo; *Flowers:* Michaels; *Zipper:* Junkitz; *Other:* Patterned papers.

Friends Are the Fabric of Life **by Cindy Knowles**

Cindy Knowles's daughter belongs to such a close-knit group of friends, she wanted to help them create a journal they could treasure over the years. With a beautiful fabric bag as a cover, the album is a place for the girls to record their dreams and project where they'll be in 10 years.

How To:

Create bags to hold the circle journals—embellish with flowers, ribbon, fabric, text and quotes. Design the journal with cardstock, fabric and patterned papers.

Cindy's Tip:

A circle journal can also become a touching tribute album. Send the album to friends or family members and ask them to add their feelings in tribute to a parent, grandparent, friend or teacher.

Supplies *Textured cardstock:* Bazzill Basics Paper; *Patterned papers:* Pebbles Inc.; *Red fabric and metal-rimmed vellum tag:* Making Memories; *Slide frame, bookplate and mini brads:* Boxer Scrapbook Productions; *Paper flowers:* Prima; *Ribbon:* May Arts, Boxer Scrapbook Productions and C.M. Offray & Son; *"Friends" vellum quotes:* The C-Thru Ruler Co.; *Computer fonts:* Selfish and Broken 15, downloaded from the Internet; LB Typewriter, "Lisa's Favorite Fonts" CD, *Creating Keepsakes; Other:* Divider tabs and toile fabric.

Blog Highlights **by Erin Lincoln**

Web logs (or "blogs") are a way to record and share your creations, musings, inspiration or day-to-day activities. Erin Lincoln ensures that her best entries won't be lost in cyberspace by printing and including them in an album that she can consult even when logged off of the computer.

How To:

Cut cardboard to approximately 12½" x 9" and score it to hold envelopes and wrap around edges. Cover cardboard with cardstock. Cut a transparency to fit over the envelopes. Drill holes through the cardboard, envelopes and transparency, and bind together with hardware. Embellish. Each month, print blog highlights and trim to fit inside envelopes.

Erin's Tip:

When working with transparencies, be careful—if you get any liquid adhesive on the surface, the smudges will be very difficult to remove.

Supplies *Textured cardstock and envelopes:* Bazzill Basics Paper; *Stickers:* Mustard Moon; *Quote:* KI Memories; *Computer sticker:* Jolee's Boutique, Sticko for EK Success; *Rub-ons and rubber stamps:* Fontwerks; *Number punch-out:* Scrapworks; *Die-cut letters:* QuicKutz; *Tacks:* Chatterbox; *Nuts, screws and washers:* The Home Depot; *Extra-long eyelets:* Making Memories; *Decoupage medium:* Mod Podge, Plaid Enterprises; *Computer font:* Keypunch, downloaded from the Internet; *Other:* Cardboard, transparency and CD.

Life in My 40s **by Michaela Young-Mitchell**

Have you faced major changes or overcome serious obstacles during one period in your life? As she entered her 40s, Michaela Young-Mitchell saw remarkable changes in her personal, professional and creative life. A collage shadow box is not only a constant reminder of the adjustments, but also a display of their positive results.

How To:

Paint and embellish a frame and letters. Adhere photos and memorabilia. Journal in magnetic booklets and on tags, then decorate and adhere.

Michaela's Tip:

Make the project quick and easy by using the pre-cut collage mat that comes with the frame. Fill the openings with photos and journaling, then add memorabilia and accents around the margins.

Supplies *Collage frame and wooden numbers:* Wal-Mart; *Ribbon:* Wal-Mart, C.M. Offray & Son, Maya Road and Michaels; *Letter stamps and stamping ink:* PSX Design; *Shipping tag:* Avery; *Magnetic journal books, puzzle words, word charm, dragonfly charm, lacing brads, paper floss, clear pocket and brads:* Karen Foster Design; *Color wash:* Adirondack Color Wash, Ranger Industries; *Chipboard letters and round bookplate:* Li'l Davis Designs; *Rub-on letters and flowers:* Making Memories; *Acrylic paint:* Plaid Enterprises; *Paper flowers:* Prima; *Stamping ink:* ColorBox Fluid Chalk, Clearsnap; *Pen:* Pigment Pro, American Crafts; *Other:* Craft wire.

Shadow Boxes
by Heather Jones

Shadow boxes are a perfect way to display three-dimensional keepsakes. Available in a variety of sizes, a shadow box is essentially a framed box that hangs on a wall, just like a photo frame. The added space creates room for bulkier mementos that won't fit into a scrapbook. You can purchase different styles and wood finishes; some even come unfinished, allowing you to customize the box to coordinate with surrounding decor or the items displayed in the box.

Basic Assembly Steps:

❶ Gather the items to be displayed.

❷ Cover the backing of the box. It's usually just a plain piece of wood that can be covered with fabric, patterned paper, paint and embellishments. It can be helpful to create a backing with batting that will provide a place to use push pins to secure display items. If you want the items to be secured permanently, adhere them directly to the wood backing using strong liquid adhesive or double-sided foam tape.

❸ Create dimension by layering items in the shadow box. Consider mounting some items on various widths of foam or wood blocks.

❹ Add additional embellishments for texture and depth.

Possible shadow box themes:

- Collections, such as sports paraphernalia, dried flowers and leaves, coins, etc.
- A baby's favorite outfit, shoes, blessing/christening outfit, etc.
- Souvenirs from a favorite trip
- Keepsakes from your wedding day
- Military medals and honors
- Work badges, IDs and uniforms for those in law enforcement and public service jobs
- Graduation mementos
- Heritage photos and heirlooms

God's Proof by Jennifer McGuire

As a tangible reminder of her faith, a durable mini album celebrates everything Jennifer McGuire holds dear. Create a similar project to accompany you on trips away from home to remind you of blessings, miracles and gifts you want to celebrate each day.

How To:

Decorate the front of a 4" x 6" album with rub-ons and twill. Combine photos, patterned papers and journaling to cover 4" x 6" pieces of cardstock for each window. Add accents to suit the theme.

Jennifer's Tip:

Keep your eyes open for sales and deals on mini albums when you're at the scrapbook or craft store. Keep several on hand—they're the perfect size for personal or gift projects.

Supplies *Album:* Target; *Patterned papers:* Making Memories and Autumn Leaves; *Rub-ons:* Autumn Leaves (flowers), Making Memories ("God's Proof"), K&Company (stitching); *Twill:* foof-a-La, Autumn Leaves; *Buttons:* Buttons Galore; *Paper flowers:* Prima; *Decorative brads:* Around the Block; *Brads:* Making Memories; *Computer font:* Arial Narrow, Microsoft Word.

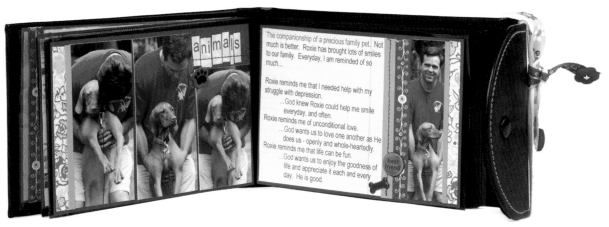

Snippets of Faith **by Joy Uzarraga**

To record the reasons she cherishes specific text from the Bible, Joy Uzarraga designed an album that explains their significance. She hopes the piece will eventually be read by her children (and grandchildren), who will discover why the verses held special meaning in her life.

How To:

Assemble your mini album and decorate the cover with patterned paper. Create an album title with stickers and your handwriting. Create pockets on each page with patterned paper. Print the text, cut it into strips and adhere them to the front of each pocket. Embellish tags, add journaling and slip into the pockets.

Joy's Tip:

Using this same process, you can make an album of quotes, song lyrics or movie lines. Use tags to journal about the meaning they have in your life.

Supplies *Mini album:* 7gypsies; *Textured cardstock:* Bazzill Basics Paper; *Patterned paper:* Scenic Route Paper Co.; *Letter stickers:* Chatterbox; *Ribbon:* May Arts; *Brads:* American Crafts and Lost Art Treasures; *Paper flowers:* Prima; *Pen:* Zig Writer, EK Success; *Computer font:* 2Peas Funky Monkey, downloaded from *www.twopeasinabucket.com.*

Blessings **by Mary Larson**

How do you remember your good fortune? Shortly after Mary Larson's father passed away, she realized just how blessed she was to have him in her life. The realization inspired her to create an album that reminds her of all she has and does not want to take for granted.

How To:

Cover an old board book with paint. Cover the front and back with fabric. Adhere ribbon to create a tabbed area at the top of each page and add a title. Embellish the cover. Design the pages with photos, patterned papers and journaling.

Mary's Tip:

Organize the project by creating a list of blessings, then finding photos associated with them. Keeping the pages simple will place the spotlight on your words, feelings and images.

Supplies *Patterned papers:* Creative Imaginations and BasicGrey; *Rubons:* 7gypsies; *File tab:* Narratives, Creative Imaginations; *Clear heart:* Heidi Swapp for Advantus; *Letter stickers:* Scrapperware, Creative Imaginations; *Metal numbers:* Li'l Davis Designs; *Chipboard letters and brads:* Making Memories; *Hemp fabric:* Artistic Scrapper, Creative Imaginations; *Ribbon and rickrack:* Michaels; *Computer fonts:* Amaretto and Chocolate Box, downloaded from the Internet; *Other:* Twill tape, fabric, trim and paint.

WWW.CREATINGKEEPSAKES.COM

For Babies, Toddlers & Teens

Even if the children you know are part of the "I want it now" generation, there's one thing they desire above all else—love. Combine the best of both worlds by giving them something you created—or better yet, created together—with a little TLC. From educational books for toddlers and decorative journals for teens to albums and treasure boxes for anyone in between, these unique pieces will make them the envy of their peers. This chapter will help you uncover imaginative, colorful ways to incorporate photos, feats and favorites into projects you can design for—or with—children of all ages.

Count Three Ways by Christa Hayden

Create a quiet book that's as huggable as it is educational. Christa Hayden used Onesies and fabric panels to design a project that features numbers up to 10 in English, Spanish and sign language. With bright colors, cute shapes and a carrying strap, it can easily become your baby's constant traveling companion.

How To:

Turn an infant's undershirt inside out and sew the sleeve and neck openings closed. Turn right side out, line with batting and sew the bottom closed. Repeat with second undershirt. Place backs together and stitch along the shoulders. Add numbers to fabric panels with iron-ons, stamps and patches. Line the panels with batting and sew together, then add ribbon and button page turners. Glue or stitch panels into book.

Christa's Tip:

Be sure any small items are attached securely and that the adhesives are non-toxic in the event your child chews on the book.

Supplies *Acrylic letters:* KI Memories; *Rubber stamps:* Purple Onion Designs, PSX Design and Technique Tuesday; *Stamping ink:* Memories, Stewart Superior Corporation; *Ribbon:* May Arts; *Buttons:* Doodlebug Design; *T-shirt transfer paper:* Avery; *Newborn outfits:* Carter's; *Embroidery floss:* DMC; *Sewing thread:* Gütemann; *Iron-on patches:* Hirschberg Schutz & Co. and Joy Insignia, Inc.; *Quilter's Polyester batting:* Carpenter Co.; *Pen:* Rub-a-Dub Laundry Marking Pen, Sanford; *Other:* Fabric and nylon strapping.

WWW.CREATINGKEEPSAKES.COM

When You Were One by Janet MacLeod

To help her one-year-old nephew remember a summer vacation they spent together, Janet MacLeod designed a playful, interactive mini album to high-light their adventures. A combination of activities, photos and captions are sure to hold his attention!

How To:

Cut cardboard to the desired size and punch holes along one side. Coat the pieces with acrylic paint. Add photos, painted details and embellishments, then add the story's text.

Janet's Tip:

Study your photos for interactive element ideas that "fit." Give pages flaps to lift, movable items attached with string, touchable fabric pieces, shiny objects or items attached with buttons—anything to involve the child in the story.

Supplies *Patterned paper:* Karen Foster Design; *Fabric swatches, tag, letters, fish buttons and foam stamps:* Making Memories; *Rub-ons:* Scrapworks (small brown); Gin-X (large brown), Imagination Project; K&Company (family words); *Acrylic paint:* Making Memories and Heidi Swapp for Advantus; *Dimensional adhesive:* Plaid Enterprises; *Photo corners and chipboard flower:* Heidi Swapp for Advantus; *Ribbon:* Heidi Swapp for Advantus (brown), KI Memories (greens and dots), Making Memories (other); *Brads:* Bazzill Basics Paper; *Sequins:* Hero Arts; *Letter stickers:* ScrapPagerz.com and www.gonescrappin.com; *Waxed floss:* Scrapworks; *Other:* Cardboard.

Dayna's Color Book *by Jenny Jackson*

Help your toddler learn colors with an album featuring photos, die cuts, stickers and more. Jenny Jackson's vibrant project also includes coordinating ribbon page turners that add interest and dimension.

How To:

Print page titles on the computer and trim. Gather colorful die cuts and add them to the appropriate pages. Use photos to help fill spaces. Design and embellish the cover with stickers, patterned paper and ribbon.

Jenny's Tip:

You don't have to use die cuts as the color shapes. Look for items representing each color in recycled magazines, greeting cards, photos and more.

Supplies *Patterned papers and brads:* Provo Craft; *Letter stickers:* American Crafts; *Ribbon:* May Arts; *Die cuts:* O'Scrap!, Cock-A-Doodle Design and Doodlebug Design; *Computer font:* Arial Black, Microsoft Word.

My Many Colored Days

by Tracey Odachowski

Tracey Odachowski loved reading the Dr. Seuss classic to her children and challenged herself to create a mini album following the theme. Using the book's actual text and photos in matching colors, the project is not only a great way to teach colors, but to discuss moods and feelings as well.

How To:

Cover chipboard to create the cover. Follow the wording of the Dr. Seuss book, adding photos to match the colors of the text. Bind the book and seal with decoupage medium. Finish the spine with ribbon.

Tracey's Tip:

If you don't have photo-editing software to help you change the color of your photos, just use regular images and let the colors of the background pages tell the story.

Supplies *Cardstock and skeleton leaf:* Stampin' Up!; *Patterned papers:* Paper Heart Studios, Junkitz, BasicGrey, Daisy D's Paper Co., Karen Foster Design, Creative Imaginations, KI Memories and Autumn Leaves; *Chipboard:* Bazzill Basics Paper; *Ribbon:* Michaels and Les Bon Ribbon; *Stickers:* KI Memories; *Acrylic paint and decoupage medium:* Plaid Enterprises; *Pen:* Permapaque, Sakura; *Star punch:* Family Treasures.

When You Were ... by Jennifer Newton

Help your children remember highlights in their lives with an annual album like the one created by Jennifer Newton. Featuring eye-catching photos, brightly colored backgrounds and large numbers filled with journaling, the book is an easy way to document achievements and interesting facts.

How To:

Create numbers and script in a word-processing program. Reverse the figures and print them onto cardstock and patterned paper. Trim with a craft knife. Layer the figures with photos and adorn the pages with the number of embellishments that corresponds with the number on each page. Add journaling.

Jennifer's Tip:

Complete all the pages of the album to make it easier to keep the album current. With the pages done, all I have to do is add the photo and journaling each year on my daughter's birthday.

Supplies *Album and patterned papers:* KI Memories; *Textured cardstock:* Bazzill Basics Paper; *Ribbon:* May Arts; *Tags:* OfficeMax; *Stamping ink:* ColorBox, Clearsnap; *Pen:* Zig Millennium, EK Success; *Paper flowers and mini brads:* Making Memories; *Colored pencils:* EK Success.

Words of Love by Vanessa Reyes

Give your children a tangible reminder of your love with an album featuring poems, quotes and journaling that show it. Vanessa Reyes designed a beautiful book to display in her home during the month of February, but it's something her family can treasure all year long.

How To:
Cut chipboard to size and cover with patterned paper. Add photos, accents and printed quotes, poems and words about love. Punch holes along the spine and attach the pages with ribbon.

Vanessa's Tip:

If you plan to display your album, select papers and embellishments that not only coordinate with your photos, but also with your home decor. Create pieces with colors you love to see.

Supplies *Patterned papers:* Scrapworks, Autumn Leaves and K&Company; *Chipboard letters and rub-ons:* Heidi Swapp for Advantus; *Canvas flowers and flourishes:* Autumn Leaves; *Leather flowers, metal word, crystal brad, mini brad, rub-ons and "I Love You" charm:* Making Memories; *Metal tab and photo turn:* 7gypsies; *Epoxy stickers:* Colorbök; *Die-cut flowers:* Legacies; *Photo corners:* Chatterbox; *Rub-on letters:* Li'l Davis Designs and Creative Imaginations; *Ribbon:* May Arts, Li'l Davis Designs, Making Memories and C.M. Offray & Son.

Live Good **by April Peterson**

Help your children think positively with an altered book filled with inspirational quotes and cherished photos. After discovering a quote book filled with colorful graphics, motivational thoughts and lots of space to add pictures, April Peterson realized the project could be something her family turns to and learns from for years to come.

How To:

Purchase a book of quotations and remove several of the pages to accommodate photos. Find images that relate to the quotes. Place some photos directly on the existing pages or design new pages to adhere inside the book.

April's Tip:

If you're going to create additional pages to place inside the album, use mostly "flat" embellishments and techniques (like machine-stitching) so the album won't be too bulky to close.

Supplies *Patterned papers and vellum:* Déjà Views, The C-Thru Ruler Co.; *Ribbon:* Making Memories and May Arts; *Stamping ink:* ColorBox, Clearsnap; *Corner rounder:* EK Success.

| WWW.CREATINGKEEPSAKES.COM

Seattle by Sue Thomas

Do you travel a lot? If your children are often upset about being "left behind," design a coaster album to share your experiences, as Sue Thomas did. After a trip to Seattle, Sue created the special album to show her daughter what she had seen and done. The project's size and durability allows her daughter to take it to school to share with friends.

How To:

Add text and photos to chipboard coasters. Punch a hole and attach coasters to the metal ring. Embellish with a shrink-plastic tag and ribbon.

Sue's Tip:

Size all photos to the same dimensions to simplify page design and text placement.

Supplies *Textured cardstock:* Bazzill Basics Paper; *Coasters:* Cloud 9 Design; *Ring clip:* Provo Craft; *Computer fonts:* AL Capone and AL Sandra, downloaded from *www.twopeasinabucket.com; Other:* Shrink plastic and ribbon.

All About My Cousins **by Renee Foss**

If your siblings live far away, helping your children get to know each other can be difficult. Renee Foss solved the problem with an album for her one-year-old niece that introduces cousins through pictures and personal journaling. By incorporating numerous colors, shapes, words and textures, the album also doubles as a learning tool.

How To:

Use a craft knife to remove book pages from the spine. Add patterned papers and photos to the pages and embellish with letters, ribbon, rub-ons and more. Journal on transparencies and attach with spray adhesive. Punch holes along each page and add eyelets. Attach pages with binder rings adorned with ribbon.

Renee's Tip:

When adding ribbon or other embellishments to the binder rings, be sure to leave a little space (rather than completely filling the rings with ribbon) so the book can be opened and closed easily.

Supplies *Board book:* Pixie Press; *Patterned papers, tag and label stickers, buttons, brads, ribbon, die cuts and stickers:* SEI; *Rub-ons and letter stickers:* BasicGrey; *Bookplate, metal-rimmed tags, chipboard tag, eyelets and small rub-on letters:* Making Memories; *Ribbon:* May Arts; *Waxed floss:* Scrapworks; *Clear letters:* Heidi Swapp for Advantus; *Vinyl letter stickers:* Li'l Davis Designs; *Staples:* EK Success; *Clips:* Rob and Bob Studio, Provo Craft; *Metal charms:* American Traditional Designs; *Computer font:* Folks, downloaded from the Internet; *Other:* Binder rings and transparency.

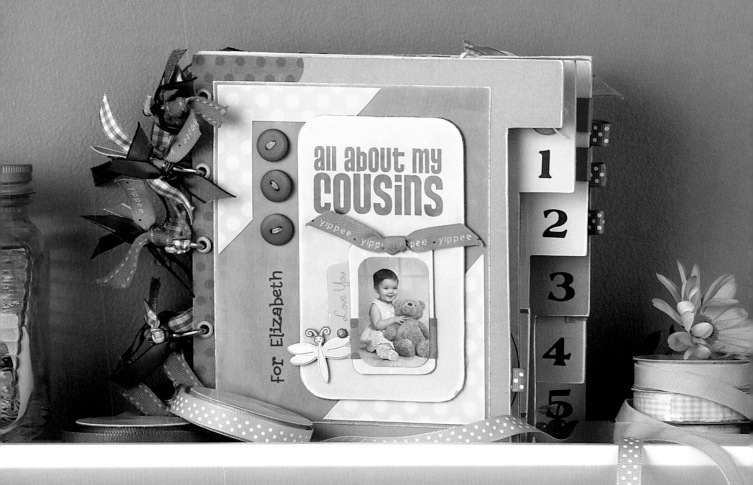

Surprise! by Sande Brown

To commemorate her daughter's birthday, Sande Brown created a special album that recounts all the events of the celebration. The book is kept in a curio cabinet where her daughter can look at it whenever she likes.

How To:

Purchase an album and decorate the spine with ribbon. Cut paper to fit the cover, stitch on rickrack and adhere to the cover with decoupage medium. Create titles for the album and pages with rubber stamps and paint. Add photos, journaling and embellishments.

Sande's Tip:

Though you may have a lot of photos you want to include, don't forget to journal—it adds to the interest and meaning of the book.

Supplies *Ribbon:* May Arts; *Rubber stamps and tiles:* Technique Tuesday; *Acrylic paint:* Making Memories; *Photo turns and fasteners:* Boxer Scrapbook Productions; *Other:* Paper clips.

Way Hip by Kim Kesti

Is your child a pack rat? Design an album like Kim Kesti's, complete with envelopes and pockets to house notes, stickers, memorabilia and other tidbits. Tell your teen to fill the pages with her most cherished treasures—the project can serve as a mini time capsule of what she loves today!

How To:
Cover the inside and outside of an album with patterned paper. Embellish the cover. Add patterned papers and keepsake envelopes to the inside pages. Add titles and teen's memorabilia.

Kim's Tip:
Save time by measuring the album pages and cutting and adhering all the background papers. Then go through and add all the pockets, titles and so on. Assembling in stages makes the process go more quickly.

Supplies *Album:* 7gypsies; *Patterned papers and rub-on letters:* Gin-X, Imagination Project; *Chipboard letters:* Li'l Davis Designs; *Rubber stamps:* Fontwerks; *Cardstock stickers:* Provo Craft; *Keepsake envelopes:* Karen Foster Design; *Ribbon:* May Arts; *Knob:* Rusty Pickle; *Hinge:* Daisy D's Paper Co.; *Acrylic paint:* Making Memories; *Stamping ink:* Ranger Industries.

WWW.CREATINGKEEPSAKES.COM

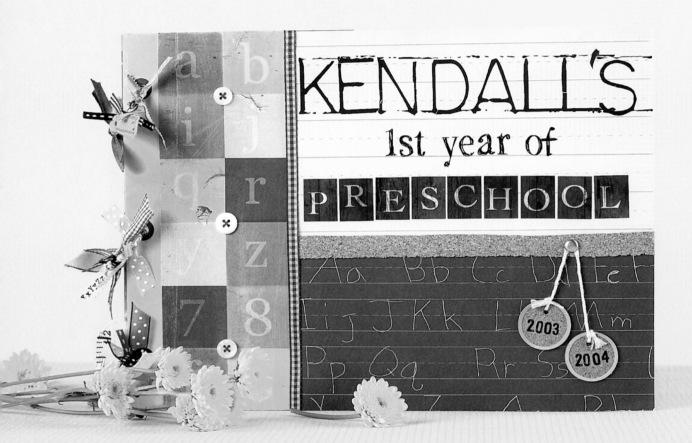

Preschool **by Vicki Harvey**

Albums about your child's school year are perfect for saving memories ... but what to do with all the memorabilia? Vicki Harvey mixed envelopes with traditional album pages to hold all of the certificates, notes and more that her children accumulate from school.

How To:

Punch holes in document envelopes and several sheets of cardstock. Attach envelopes and cardstock with binder rings. Embellish the cover and pages with patterned papers, photos, memorabilia and accents. Add ribbon to the binder rings.

Vicki's Tip:

If you have a lot of memorabilia to store, create a book made up of all envelopes. Decorate them with photos and accents just as you would the cardstock pages.

Supplies *Patterned papers:* Daisy D's Paper Co., Making Memories, Rusty Pickle, Carolee's Creations, My Mind's Eye, Scenic Route Paper Co., Autumn Leaves and K&Company; *Rub-on letters:* Autumn Leaves and Scenic Route Paper Co.; *Letter stickers and library card:* Daisy D's Paper Co.; *Cork tags:* Creative Imaginations; *Number stickers:* Mustard Moon; *Brads, cork paper, red, tan, black and green gingham ribbon, measuring-tape twill and letter twill:* Creative Imaginations; *Photo corners:* Kolo; *Metal-rimmed tags:* Making Memories; *Paper clip and epoxy letter stickers:* Li'l Davis Designs; *File Folder:* Autumn Leaves; *Small tag:* Avery; *Rub-on letters:* Chatterbox; *Pen:* Pigment Pro, American Crafts; *Index tabs and gaffer tape:* 7gypsies; *Measuring-tape stickers and "K" typewriter sticker:* EK Success; *Rub-on phrase:* Melissa Frances; *Rub-on letters:* Heidi Swapp for Advantus; *Rub-on "K" and green twill:* Scenic Route Paper Co.; *Conchos:* Scrapworks; *Label tape:* Dymo; *Red, black and blue stitched ribbon and green polka-dot ribbon:* May Arts; *Envelopes and binding rings:* Office Depot; *Computer font:* Teletype, downloaded from the Internet; *Other:* Buttons.

School Days **by Kristi Barnes**

Because Kristi Barnes's family has moved several times during her daughters' elementary school years, she wanted a way for them to remember their previous teachers and friends. A grade-by-grade mini book showcases school photos of each daughter, giving them a chance to reminisce and compare themselves at the same age.

How To:

Create a file tab for each page in a small board book. Cover the pages with cardstock and add photos and journaling. Embellish with patterned papers, stickers, clips and ribbon.

Kristi's Tip:

Adhere the file tabs before covering the pages with patterned paper so the edges will be concealed. Once the pages are covered, lightly sand the sides and corners to help the patterned paper better fit the book.

Supplies *Board book:* C&T Publishing; *Patterned papers and sticker word strips:* Bo-Bunny Press; *Memo cards:* 7gypsies; *Metal tag:* Provo Craft; *Ribbon:* May Arts; *Apple die cut:* Sizzix, Provo Craft; *Computer font:* CK Constitution, "Fresh Fonts" CD, *Creating Keepsakes; Other:* Paper clips and stamping ink.

WWW.CREATINGKEEPSAKES.COM

My School Memories   by **Mary Larson**

Mary Larson turned a cigar box into a cool container where her son can store trinkets and tidbits he collects at school. The box also holds another treasure—a smaller decorated tin to save his friends' school portraits.

How To:

Cover a cigar box with patterned papers. Attach letters, a framed photo and ribbon. Inside, cover the lid with patterned paper and add rub-ons and ribbon.

Mary's Tip:

To help the paper adhere smoothly to the box, consider using a Xyron machine or spray adhesive. You can also use a brayer to flatten the paper and remove any bubbles.

MY SCHOOL MEMORIES BOX
Supplies *Patterned papers:* Bo-Bunny Press and Carolee's Creations; *Chipboard letters and frame:* Li'l Davis Designs; *Patches:* Memories Complete; *Rub-ons:* Doodlebug Design; *Ribbon:* May Arts; *Box and tin:* Recollections; *Other:* Rickrack.

Altered Journals
by Heather Jones

Altering journals is a snap. Pre-bound books can easily be converted into stylish photo albums, scrapbooks, quote books, inspiration journals or memento-keepers. The best part? You don't need to bother with binding a book—it's already been done for you!

Follow these three easy steps to alter a journal:

① Begin with a plain journal or blank composition book.
② Collect images that reflect your chosen theme.
③ Place the images on the cover of the journal. Use decoupage medium or laminating film to secure the items.

Now that you've got the technique down, check out the following ideas for inspiration!

- Cover your journal with fabric and other accessories.
- Get a natural, earthy look with sticks, stones, corrugated paper and handmade paper.
- Create a guest sign-in book for a wedding reception, and include photos and comments from the happy couple.
- Create pockets on the interior pages by adhering a piece of cardstock. Insert flat souvenirs and mementos.
- Dress up a date book/planner using time-themed accents.
- Use photos of a trip, map-patterned paper, quote rub-ons and ephemera to create a travel journal for documenting details of your trip.
- Cover an album with favorite details to celebrate a fashion or hobby, such as a collection.
- Use scans from newspaper clippings, yearbook pages and school logos to create an altered journal with team spirit.

Your Yearbook by Laurie Stamas

When designing an album for a graduate—who happened to be editor of the school yearbook—Laurie Stamas designed multiple yearbook-inspired tribute pages. In addition to high-school achievements, the book covers images and accolades from her entire school career, along with space for her family to write well-wishes, yearbook style.

How To:

Embellish the album cover with stamps, iron-ons and clear letters. Add a tassel and ribbon to the spine. Add photos and journaling. Cover the inside front and back covers with white cardstock that family members and friends can sign.

Laurie's Tip:

Start early on the project and keep it simple. The book doesn't have to contain every accomplishment from the graduate's school experience, just the highlights.

Supplies *Album and photo corners:* Canson; *Patterned papers:* Chatterbox, Carolee's Creations and K&Company; *Textured cardstock:* Bazzill Basics Paper; *Clear stamps and accessories:* Technique Tuesday; *Rubber stamps:* Fontwerks and Hero Arts; *Woven school labels:* me & my BIG ideas; *Photo turns, tabs and shaped clips:* 7gypsies; *Printed twill:* foof-a-La, Autumn Leaves; *Stamping ink:* Clearsnap and Ranger Industries; *Embossing powder:* Stampendous!; *Plastic letters and embellishments:* Heidi Swapp for Advantus; *Acrylic paint, brads, ribbon, bookplate, tags, fabric stickers, chipboard letters, metal embellishments, jump rings and woven labels:* Making Memories; *Rub-ons:* Heidi Swapp for Advantus, Autumn Leaves, Making Memories, Scrapworks and Sandylion; *Iron-on letters:* Prym-Dritz; *Clear plastic letters:* Heidi Grace Designs; *Fasteners:* Magic Scraps; *Chipboard embellishments, mini bottle-cap numbers and metal stencil numbers:* Li'l Davis Designs; *Paper flowers:* Prima; *Laser die cut:* Deluxe Designs; *Label tape:* Dymo; *Pens:* American Crafts, EK Success and Sanford; *Computer font:* Times New Roman, Microsoft Word; *Other:* Tassel, felt stick-on numbers, large report card envelope, ribbon, library pockets and tags.

H by **Heather Preckel**

Anyone would love a cute monogram like this to hang on his or her wall. Heather Preckel designed one for herself based on a plaque she created for her daughter's room. When designing yours, accessorize the basic black with ribbon ties to coordinate with where you will display it.

How To:
Cover a wood monogram with patterned-paper strips. Attach the monogram to the black cardstock background with dimensional foam tape. Add writing with a white gel pen. Hang with string adorned with ribbon ties.

Heather's Tip:
To give the cardstock added weight, back it with a smaller piece of sturdy cardboard before hanging.

Supplies *Textured cardstock:* Bazzill Basics Papers; *Patterned paper and monogram:* A2Z Essentials; *Ribbon:* May Arts, Michaels and C.M. Offray & Son; *Staples:* Target; *Pen:* Uni-ball, Sanford.

M by **Jamie Harper**

What better way for Santa to find your child's stocking than to include a personalized monogram near the hook? Jamie Harper suggests choosing paint colors that match your "everyday" decor (rather than those that represent the holidays) so you can use it all year to hang backpacks, jackets and more.

How To:
Paint the monogram and backboard in contrasting colors. Trace the letter onto patterned paper and trim. Cover the wood letter with white glue and smooth paper onto it. Embellish with ribbon, fabric and twill letters. Attach the paper to the letter with strong liquid adhesive and allow to dry overnight.

Jamie's Tip:
You don't have to make the project elaborate—if you don't want to add the fabric or embellishments, you can simply decorate the monogram with paint.

Supplies *Patterned paper, monogram letter and twill letters:* Carolee's Creations; *Ribbon:* Making Memories; *Paint:* Dutch Boy; *Fabric:* Jo-Ann Stores; *Other:* Wood and hook.

Smile by Shelley Laming

Give your teen something to smile about with a locker mirror that's a step above the norm. Featuring acrylic word tiles and letter magnets, the cute addition is sure to keep Shelley Laming's daughter and her locker mate grinning between classes.

How To:

Use adhesive dots to attach tiles and letters along the top and bottom of a magnetized mirror. Embellish a tag and add along with a flower charm. Hang the tag from one of the letters.

Shelley's Tip:

Locker mirrors aren't just for girls. Adapt the project for a boy by using a more masculine color scheme and omitting the hanging tag.

Supplies *Acrylic tiles:* KI Memories; *Tag:* SilverCrow Creations; *Other:* Mirror, charm and refrigerator magnets.

A Girl Thing by Vicki Harvey

When the room her daughters share needed a bit of decoration, Vicki Harvey designed a custom frame and mat to showcase a darling photo of the pair. Patterned paper is an ideal material to revamp plain frames and complement any decor.

How To:

Sand and paint a recycled frame. Add strips of patterned paper with decoupage medium. Embellish the photo mat with strips of paper. Add a flower, ribbon and rub-on words.

Vicki's Tip:

If you want to add bulky embellishments to the photo mat, simply remove the glass from the frame to accommodate them.

Supplies *Patterned papers:* Making Memories; *Rub-on phrase:* Melissa Frances; *Ribbon:* May Arts; *Acrylic paint:* Delta Technical Coatings; *Chipboard circle:* Bazzill Basics Paper; *Flower:* Michaels.

Tori by Teri Fode

Upon hearing that all the girls in her daughter's class use locker mirrors after PE, Teri Fode put her scrapbooking skills to good use to create a colorful rendition. Adhering a magnet to the back of this once-ordinary hand mirror helps it cling to the locker door.

How To:

Paint the mirror frame with acrylic paint and seal with decoupage medium. Embellish with rub-ons, flowers and ribbon. Attach a magnet to the back.

Teri's Tips:

Before painting the mirror's frame, add painter's tape around the edges of the mirror to avoid getting paint or sealer on it. Also, cleaning the mirror first will help rub-ons adhere better.

Supplies *Mirror:* Target; *Ribbon:* KI Memories and American Crafts; *Acrylic paint:* Delta Technical Coatings; *Decoupage medium:* Mod Podge, Plaid Enterprises; *Pen:* Gelly Roll, Sakura; *Paper flowers:* Prima; *Letter stickers:* Doodlebug Design.

Helen and Hunter by Christa Hayden

As a Christmas gift to her children, Christa Hayden created a DVD of the year's highlights so they could watch and reminisce. The thoughtful present was made even more special when enclosed in a bright, custom-made DVD cover that showcases a great photo from the year.

How To:
Remove and measure a DVD box insert, then discard. Cut patterned paper to size and decorate with photos, punches, letters and flowers. Place the pages inside the DVD cover.

Christa's Tip:
Be sure to measure correctly and use only "flat" embellishments to help the insert fit nicely inside the DVD cover.

Supplies *Textured cardstock:* Prism Papers; *Patterned paper:* My Mind's Eye; *Chipboard flower and metal monogram:* Making Memories; *Lace photo frame:* QuicKutz; *Pens:* Faber-Castell and Sakura; *Circle punch:* EK Success; *Other:* DVD case.

Victory by Miley Johnson

Here's an unforgettable addition to any athlete's trophy case—a CD of the season's highlights stored in a commemorative mini album. Miley Johnson obtained radio and television highlights from her stepson's undefeated baseball season and placed the CD in an accordion book that also showcases photos from the championship year.

How To:
Add photos and accents to a film reel. Cover the pages of an accordion booklet with patterned papers. Punch film strips to attach to the pages, then add photos and stencils. Attach the pages with a large brad.

Miley's Tip:
A decorative CD holder would also make a great wedding or baby shower gift. You could also burn a CD with love songs and include them in a little album for your sweetheart!

Supplies *Film reel:* Urbanartsandcrafts.com; *Patterned papers:* Chatterbox; *Barcodes:* Mystic Press; *Definitions and brads:* Making Memories; *Twill:* 7gypsies; *Letter stickers:* Creative Imaginations; *Film punch:* Family Treasures; *Accordion booklet:* Autumn Leaves; *Computer font:* Times New Roman, Microsoft Word; *Other:* Stencils.

Beads and Baubles **by Kim Kesti**

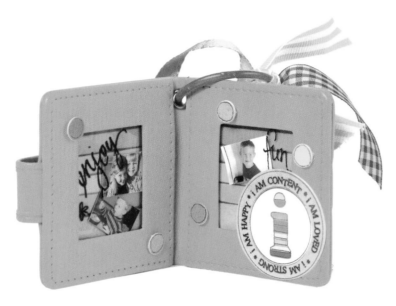

Help your teen (or even yourself) carry a couple of your scrapbooking creations with her wherever she goes. Kim Kesti incorporated two miniature scrapbook pages into a colorful photo holder turned keychain album adorned with ribbon and beads.

How To:

Punch a hole in the photo holder and add an eyelet. Attach the key ring and add ribbon. Insert mini scrapbook pages inside the album and embellish the cover with a sticker and monogram. Add beads and wire to the key ring.

Kim's Tip:

Even if you don't scrapbook, you can create a keychain. Instead of designing mini scrapbook pages to fit inside the album, just trim and slip photos into the spaces.

Supplies *Patterned paper and cardstock stickers:* Christina Cole for Provo Craft; *Epoxy letters and eyelet:* Creative Imaginations; *Acrylic letter:* KI Memories; *Ribbon:* May Arts; *Key ring:* Junkitz; *Beads:* Blue Moon Designs; *Photo holder:* Crate & Barrel.

Eliza **by Shelley Laming**

Though Shelley Laming designed her decorative keychain as an adornment to hang from a picture frame or bulletin board, imagine how well the personalized gift would go over when connected to your teen's first set of car keys!

How To:

Add name and accents to small acrylic frames. Attach frames with a length of ribbon. Add a key ring and accents.

Shelley's Tip:

Embellish both sides of the frames so they'll look good from all angles. To make the project easier, simply add small photos to the frames instead of patterned paper.

Supplies *Pattered papers:* My Mind's Eye and Anna Griffin; *Die-cut sticker:* KI Memories; *Metal letter charm:* Making Memories; *Stamping ink:* ColorBox, Clearsnap; *Heart bead:* The Bead Store; *Ribbon:* May Arts; *Other:* Tiny tag, key ring, frames and earring.

Taylor's Stuff by Allison Landy

Though she's only a freshman, Allison Landy's daughter has already accumulated quite a stash of memorabilia from high school. In addition to serving as a place to store these belongings, this customized box is also decorated in a style that reflects Taylor's interests and personality.

How To:

Paint a box with acrylic paint, then coat with a colored decoupage medium. Adhere patterned paper and seal with decoupage medium. Add stamped images, rub-ons and ephemera.

Allison's Tip:

The binder clips along the outside of the box allow the recipient to hang whatever fits the fad or mood of the moment.

Supplies *Patterned papers:* Autumn Leaves and Scrapworks; *Letter stamps:* Brooklyn Bridge and Technique Tuesday; *Stamping ink:* StazOn, Tsukineko; *Rub-on letters:* Making Memories (black) and KI Memories (green); *Rub-ons and die cut:* Autumn Leaves; *Paper flowers:* Prima; *Brads:* The Happy Hammer (small) and Making Memories (large); *Chipboard letter:* BasicGrey; *Dyed twill:* Scenic Route Paper Co.; *Decoupage medium:* Mod Podge, Plaid Enterprises; *Other:* Mini binder clips and acrylic paint.

Mykiah's Treasures by Kimberly Lund

From charm bracelets to friends' notes to ticket stubs, every child has a host of treasures. This photo box by Kimberly Lund is the perfect place to store riches big and small. The customized lid clearly defines who the box belongs to ... and warns others to keep out!

How To:

Create a layout with photos and digital elements. Send the layout to a photo-processing website that will print it onto a ceramic tile and place on a hardwood box.

Kimberly's Tip:

To personalize the box even more, add text to the picture with photo-editing software before creating the box.

Supplies *Software:* Adobe Photoshop Elements 3.0, Adobe Systems; *Digital elements:* Kristie David, downloaded from *www.theshabbyshoppe.com*; *Virtual photographer filter on photo:* Downloaded from *www.optikvervelabs.com*; *Photo gift creation:* Downloaded from *www.snapfish.com*; *Digital letter:* Lyndsay Riches, downloaded from *www.scrapbook-bytes.com*; *Computer font:* CAC Shoshoni Brush, downloaded from the Internet.

A to Z Journal **by Tracy Miller**

Give your child the space to recollect, journal and dream. Tracy Miller designed a cool journal for her daughter to use one day—unlined pages afford a space to write, doodle or add photos, while themes will give her thoughts an inspirational nudge.

How To:

Embellish the cover with rubber stamps, chipboard, ribbon and a title. Cover the inside front and back covers with patterned paper. Add an introduction to the inside front cover. Title each page, then add tags to serve as an index.

Tracy's Tip:

Want to make a journal in a fraction of the time? Just purchase a premade journal and list the topic ideas at the top of each page!

COVER
Supplies *Chipboard album, chipboard coaster and epoxy letters:* Li'l Davis Designs; *Letter stamps and shape:* Fontwerks; *Ribbon:* Scrapworks and unknown; *Stamping ink:* StazOn, Tsukineko.

Get Creative!
by Heather Jones

It's easy to get overwhelmed by all the projects, memorabilia, notes and cards kids accumulate—not to mention the mountain of photos taken of them at each stage! In addition to the creative ideas shown in this chapter, why not consider some of these ideas to not only preserve but organize their paper trail? A bonus? You can get your kids in on the fun, and each project requires just a few simple supplies.

Use these ideas to spark your creativity:

At your child's next birthday party, leave out a stack of cardstock, markers, stickers and an instant camera (Polaroid or digital attached to a printer). After taking a photo of each guest, let them create scrapbook pages in honor of your child.

When the party is over, simply assemble the book and you'll have a wonderful memento for your child.

Use decorative molding and corkboard to create a bulletin board for your child to display her projects.

Create a pop-up book using photos of your child and his friends. Let the child write the story and help him cut out photos and assemble the book.

Help your child decorate cheap wooden crates with craft supplies, scrapbooking materials, paint, stamps, etc. Once complete, use the bins to store toys, projects and more.

Consider these possible themes for albums and projects:

- ABC Books
- All About Me at Age …
- Color Book
- Day Trips
- Family Traditions
- Holidays
- When I Grow Up …
- Parties

- Pets
- Grandparents
- School Achievements, Photos or Projects
- Sports
- My Family
- A Favorite Family Story

only you can be you
be an
ORIGINAL
and we like it that way

a journal a to z

Dear Diary **by Erin Lincoln**

How do you feel when you re-read your old diaries? Creatively refurbishing a plain address book to reveal some of her teenage diary entries and her take on them now, Erin Lincoln hopes to show the project to her "future girls" and prove that everything will be alright when it comes to preteen angst.

How To:

Remove pages from an address book, but reserve one to serve as a template. Cut the sides and purse flap from cardstock and adhere to the back. Cover the outside of the book with patterned papers. Create a handle with a pipe bracket and brads. Embellish the purse flap. Create pages using the original page to measure hole placement. Close the flap with double-sided Velcro.

Erin's Tip:

Practice with decoupage medium to get a feel for it before creating your project. Learn how much or how little to use to avoid bubbling and warping, for example.

Supplies *Album:* Hallmark; *Patterned papers:* Treehouse Memories, Provo Craft and Paperfever; *Rub-ons:* Rusty Pickle, Fontwerks, KI Memories and Heidi Swapp for Advantus; *Quote sticker:* KI Memories; *Large brads:* Karen Foster Design; *Small brads and buttons:* Making Memories and American Crafts; *Metal flowers:* Making Memories; *Tabs:* QuicKutz; *Pipe bracket:* The Home Depot; *Concho:* Scrapworks; *Punches:* EK Success; *Decoupage medium:* Mod Podge, Plaid Enterprises; *Computer fonts:* Times New Roman, Microsoft Word; ZapFDingbats BT, downloaded from the Internet; *Other:* Craft wire and Velcro.

This Is My Life by Katherine Brooks

Wouldn't you have loved a diary this cool when you were a teen? With a monogram, flower and funky embellishments, the journal designed by Katherine Brooks is a space where anyone would be proud to write her thoughts.

How To:
Cover the front and back of an album with patterned paper. Embellish the cover with a chipboard letter, beads, glaze, rub-ons and ribbon.

Katherine's Tip:
Consider keeping a journal yourself! Jotting down notes of day-to-day events and thoughts is a great way to remember things for future scrapbook pages.

Supplies *Patterned paper:* K&Company; *Tag template:* Deluxe Designs; *Gaffer tape and sticker:* 7gypsies; *Rubber stamp:* Wendi Speciale Designs; *Rub-ons:* Autumn Leaves and 7gypsies; *Index tabs:* Avery; *Stamping ink:* ColorBox, Clearsnap; *Acrylic paint:* Delta Technical Coatings; *Walnut ink:* Fiber Scraps; *Chipboard letter:* BasicGrey; *Foam stamps and eyelets:* Making Memories; *Label tape:* Dymo; *Dimensional adhesive:* Diamond Glaze, JudiKins; *Other:* Flower, ribbon, key and micro beads.

Memories by Tena Sprenger

Does your teen have enough activities, appointments and achievements to cause your planner to overflow? To help her daughter keep track of everything she's got going on, Tena Sprenger designed a custom calendar that doubles as a keepsake book for milestones and photos.

How To:
Create a backboard for the calendar by covering corrugated cardboard with patterned paper. Create the calendar by nesting and stitching embellished file folders. Embellish each page with a mini calendar, photos and notes. Attach pages to the backboard with brads.

Tena's Tip:
An easy way to "wallpaper" surfaces with paper is with a glue stick and brayer. Completely coat the back of the paper with adhesive, place it on a flat surface, then run a brayer over it to help it sit securely without bubbles and wrinkles.

Supplies *Patterned papers:* Captured Elements and Making Memories; *Twill:* C.M. Offray & Son; *Textured cardstock and brads:* Bazzill Basics Paper; *Mini calendars:* Basics Paper Company; *Waxed linen thread:* Lineco; *Vinyl letters:* Deflecto; *Stamping ink:* Ranger Industries; *Metal disk:* Provo Craft; *Mini brads:* Lasting Impressions for Paper; *Rubber stamps:* Postmodern Design; *Other:* Manila folders, corrugated cardboard and staples.

WWW.CREATINGKEEPSAKES.COM

Glossary of Terms

Whether you're a beginner, intermediate or advanced scrapbooker, you may stumble upon a crafting expression or idea that's new to you. So if you're searching for the definition of a basic scrapbooking tool, topic or technique, consult the following list:

Accent

An item, premade or handmade, used to "dress up" a scrapbook layout. Anything from a sticker or a pressed flower to a decorative tag or metal mesh qualifies as an "accent."

Accordion Album

A two-sided album made of a continuous sheet of paper folded back and forth "accordion-style." The album expands to show multiple pages at once.

Acid-Free

Products designated as "acid free" have a pH factor of 7 or greater. Acid-free products, such as cardstock, are used on scrapbook pages where contact with acidity could cause or hasten a photo's deterioration process.

Acrylic Paint

A water-based, synthetic paint designed to dry quickly. Can be thinned with water for color washes, dry-brushed, texturized or used to change or enhance the color of accents.

Adhesive

Products that affix photos, paper or embellishments to the background page, including adhesive dots, dimensional tape or dots, double-stick tape, glue sticks, liquid glues, photo splits, sprays and tabs. Some adhesives are better for particular applications than others. Many varieties are available in both permanent and repositionable versions (which allow you to lift and move the item repeatedly after the adhesive has dried).

Aging

A method used to give cardstock, paper, embellishments or photos an antiquated or distressed appearance. Sanding, crumpling, inking, dry-brushing or staining with dyes or inks can all give items an aged look.

Album

A three-ring, strap-hinge or post-bound book that is used, in conjunction with page protectors, to hold completed scrapbook pages. Other styles, such as spiral-bound and mini albums, typically feature permanently affixed pages that can serve as page backgrounds.

Altered

When the appearance of an item (anything from patterned paper to a composition book to a compact disc) is transformed with inks, paints, mediums or collage.

Antiquing Medium

A semi-transparent glaze in brown or earth tones applied to an item to create an aged, darkened appearance.

Archival

Products and materials that have been shown to have a safe amount of acidic and buffered content and that will not harm photos over time.

Batting

Sheets or layers of cotton or synthetic material used for lining quilts.

Board Book

Used for altering, a board book is a small book with heavy cardboard pages. Scrapbookers can alter printed children's board books or purchase blank board books to alter.

Bone Folder

A curved tool designed to help make crisp folds and creases in cardstock. Can also be used to score or burnish materials.

Book Cloth

Woven fabric infused with a protective coating that is used for covering books.

Border

A decorative design used to adorn the edge or periphery of a layout.

Brad

A metallic, colored or matte fastener that can also serve decorative purposes. Brad "tops" can be circular, shaped or ornate, and their double prongs should be inserted through the materials to be held together and then spread open in back to secure.

Brass Template

A small, thin piece of brass with decorative shapes cut out of it to be used for dry-embossing or stenciling.

Brayer

A type of roller (available in different densities, from soft foam to hard rubber) that can be used to spread ink or mediums onto cardstock. Brayers can also be used to burnish materials or to create artistic resist and textured effects.

Burnish

To rub a material with a tool to either smooth, compact or set it. Materials can be burnished with a bone folder, a brayer or even a Popsicle stick.

Circle Journal

An album circulated among a group of friends. Each participant adds her own decorative pages and sends the album to the next person in the group.

Chalk

Available in a range of color palettes and applied with a sponge applicator, cotton ball, brush or fingertip, chalk can be used to apply a soft pastel color to backgrounds or images. Chalks are also ideal for shading and filling in stamped images.

Chalk Ink

Whether it's a dye or pigment type, chalk ink produces a powdery, muted finish. Many varieties allow stamped images to stand out on dark cardstock.

Chipboard

Thick paper board that can be used as a sturdy background, a mini-album cover or a frame for a shadow box.

Clip Art

Ready-made artwork or images, often obtained from books or Internet sites, that can be cut and pasted or printed to serve as embellishments or paper-piecing patterns.

Coil Bound

Utilizes a binding with a single or double-loop wire or plastic coil that fits into holes drilled in the pages. See Spiral Bound.

Collage

Using a variety of items, from memorabilia and mixed media to photos, clip art or stamped images, to create a single decorative accent, cover or background. Items can be glued in place or adhered with a glaze or decoupage medium.

Color Wash

Applying a thin layer of watercolors, dye or watered-down acrylic paint to add a subtle tint of color to backgrounds or accents.

Composition Book

A bound notebook, typically 9¾" x 7¾", with cardboard covers and white, lined filler paper.

Concho

A small metal piece. Open styles can be used to "frame" images or accents, while closed, decorative shapes can be used as fasteners. Some varieties are also referred to as "nailheads."

Corner Rounder

A hand-held punch designed to remove the sharp, 90-degree corner from a photo, leaving a curved, blunt edge.

Craft Knife

A lightweight knife, usually the size of a pen, with a pointed blade used to cut paper and cardstock.

Cropping

Trimming a photo to make it more appealing by changing its size or composition or by eliminating unnecessary or cluttered backgrounds. In addition, the act of scrapbooking is also referred to as "cropping."

Decoupage

Adhering memorabilia, illustrations or pictures to a background layer by layer, resulting in a decorative collage. A clear glue or glaze is used to seal and protect the finished piece.

Decoupage Medium

A clear glaze used to apply cut-out paper or fabric pieces to a surface. Decoupage medium acts as a protective sealer, glue and varnish.

Die Cut

A shape cut with a professional or personal press using a metal, plastic or wood die. Dies, which feature sharp steel rules to cut the shape, are available in a variety of shapes, letters and sizes.

Dimensional Adhesive

A liquid glue or glaze that retains its dimension as it dries. Most can be stamped into for textured looks or to create faux wax seals.

Distressing

Using items, such as sandpaper or steel wool, or techniques, such as crinkling and inking, to create an old, worn look on paper, wood, fabric, etc.

Dry-Brushing

Adding texture or a wash of color to paper, cardstock or accents by adding acrylic paint with a stiff brush with completely dry bristles.

Dry-Embossing

The process of using a stylus and a metal or plastic template to impress a pattern into paper, creating a raised image.

Embellishment

Any type of accent, decoration or adornment used to dress up or further the theme of a layout.

Embossing Enamel

A large-granule (clear or colored) powder that is sprinkled over a wet stamped or drawn image and melted with a heat gun to product a shiny, dimensional look. Embossing enamel is thicker than embossing powder and produces textured, bumpy and cracked-glass effects.

Embossing Gun

A tool that directs hot air to a concentrated spot to speed-dry stamping ink or to melt embossing powder.

Embossing Ink

A clear or slightly tinted sticky ink designed for use with rubber stamps and embossing powder. Chalk can also be applied over the ink to produce soft designs.

Embossing Powder

Granules (clear or colored) that are sprinkled over a wet stamped or drawn image and melted with a heat gun to produce a shiny, dimensional image.

Embossing Template

A piece of brass or plastic with shapes or letters removed. Used in conjunction with a light box and stylus to create raised images.

Ephemera

Items, such as tickets, postcards or vintage images, that can be used in collage or to adorn layouts.

Epoxy

A clear medium often used to create three-dimensional embellishments.

Eyelet

A fastener with a back that must be flattened with a metal "setter" to be attached. Also known as "grommets," eyelets are available in a range of styles and colors, from the classic circle shape to themed shapes and versions with completely "closed" decorative tops.

Family Group Record

A form used to record a family group, including parents, children and children's spouses. Includes dates and places of births, marriages and deaths.

Fibers

Whether they resemble fluffy yarn, thin metallic filaments or strands of floss, these string-like embellishments are used to hang other accents, tie items together or simply add a bit of dimension to a layout.

Foam Stamps

Stamps, available in a variety of shapes and sizes, constructed of durable foam. Foam stamps are typically used with acrylic paint or stamping ink.

Foam Tape

Double-sided adhesive with a foam center that provides a strong, permanent hold and adds dimension to the item to which it is adhered.

Focal Point

An element on a layout designed or positioned to immediately catch the viewer's eye.

Fusible Tape

Double-sided, transparent, iron-on tape used to fuse two layers of fabric together without stitching.

Gel Pen

A pen with smooth-flowing, opaque metallic or colored ink. Many brands feature colored inks that are easily visible on dark cardstock.

Gesso

A water-based paint (sometimes a mixture of whiting and glue) used to prepare a surface for painting or gilding.

Glaze

A transparent medium that dries to a clear, glass-like finish. A glaze can act as an adhesive as well as add dimension to page elements.

Heat-Embossing

The process of using a heat source, such as an embossing gun, to melt embossing powder on a stamped image to create a raised, shiny effect.

Heritage Photos

Vintage, nostalgic photos that often document family, community or world history.

Hot Glue

Solid, dry glue sticks designed to be placed inside an electric gun, then heated and melted as you press a "trigger," allowing the liquid to be adhered to a variety of materials. Hot glue can also be used to create dimensional looks and faux wax seals.

Journaling

The text on a scrapbook page, which often tells the story behind the event or photos.

Jump Ring

A small metal ring used to connect decorative elements.

Jute

Durable string or thin rope typically manufactured from plant fibers.

Lamination

Sandwiching an item between two pieces of clear material in an attempt to protect or preserve it.

Layering

Overlapping items to create additional dimension, texture or visual interest.

Masking

Covering portions of an item to prevent them from being painted, chalked or inked when other sections are being colored. In stamping, an image may be masked so another can be stamped on top of it without overlap.

Matting

Placing a material such as cardstock, patterned paper or fabric behind a photo, allowing a decorative border to remain around the periphery.

Memorabilia

Materials that document or commemorate past events, such as flyers, brochures, newspaper clippings, post-cards or tickets.

Mesh

Pressure-sensitive, self-adhesive mesh paper or metal mesh and screening that can be used to add texture to layouts.

Mica

Translucent, acid-free and heat-resistant "tiles" that can be peeled apart to paper-thin consistency. Mica can be used to press or showcase images or flat embellishments.

Micro Beads

Tiny glass or plastic beads without holes, generally .5mm in size.

Mini Album

A small album that can be purchased pre-assembled or created with tags, slide mounts or folded cardstock. A mini album can be attached as a pull-out on a large scrapbook page, used as a theme book or presented as a gift.

Mixed Media

Combining two or more media (such as painting, collage, colored pencils) in a single piece of artwork.

Molding Paste

Water-soluble acrylic medium used to create a textured or embossed effect. Molding paste can be used with templates, stencils, rubber stamps, etc., and colored with chalks, paints or stamping ink.

Monogram

A single decorative letter; typically a person's initial.

Mulberry Paper

Thin, fibrous paper with rich colors that can be torn, layered or stamped. Produces a feathery edge when torn.

Museum Board

Buffered, acid-free mat board made of 100-percent cotton fibers. Designed for conservation, museum board is often used for matting fine art, valuable documents, limited-edition prints and photos.

Muslin

Sturdy, lightweight unbleached or white fabric.

Page Pebble

A clear, slightly raised accent used to create a glass-like effect over a letter, word or other image. Page pebbles are also available with a letter, word or other design embedded inside.

Page Protectors

Clear or slightly matte plastic sleeves designed to hold completed scrapbook pages. Only acid- and polypropylene-free versions should be used for archival projects.

Paper Piecing

Trimming, layering and gluing cardstock or other materials to re-create an image. Often based on a pattern, such as a picture from a tole painting or coloring book.

Paper Piercer

A metal tool with a sharp point used to punch small holes in cardstock for hand-stitching or to insert fasteners. Also used for a form of paper crafting in which holes are punched into a vellum-like material for an elegant appearance.

Paper Punch

A small tool constructed of metal and plastic that punches through cardstock, paper or metal to produce a decorative shape.

Paper Trimmer

A tool designed to trim the edges from cardstock, paper or photos. Available in personal, guillotine or rotary styles, some trimmers even feature interchangeable blades that produce decorative edges.

Pedigree Chart

A chart that shows the relationship between a person and his or her direct-line ancestors, e.g. from you to your parents, to your grandparents, to your great-grandparents, etc.

Photo-Editing Software

Computer software that allows you to crop, edit and organize photos.

Photo Turn

A flat metal piece attached with an eyelet or brad that features a point that rotates to secure a photo or flat embellishment.

Pocket

A page element created to hold memorabilia or additional photos on a page.

Polymer Clay

Clay that is pliable at room temperature, allowing it to be formed, stamped or impressed. Some varieties need to be baked to dry and set, while others simply air dry. Once hardened, items can be painted, sanded or polished.

Post-Bound

Scrapbook album that features two or three short metal posts that interlock and hold top-loading page protectors. Most brands can be expanded by adding post extensions.

Printable Canvas

A thin, but sturdy material designed to run through ink-jet printers without wrinkling or buckling.

Repositionable Adhesive

Adhesive that allows an item to be removed and re-stuck numerous times.

Resist

A resist is created when one ink "resists" being colored over by another. The effect is most dramatic when the color underneath is lighter than the color(s) on top. Used on dark paper, resist ink creates a watermark look.

Rub-Ons

Letters, numbers, words and images that can be rubbed on to cardstock and other surfaces with a burnisher.

Sanding

Using sandpaper or a wire brush to distress and scrape away the top layer of patterned paper, white-core cardstock or pre-printed accents.

Scoring

Using a special blade or sharp object to impress a line into cardstock for a crisp fold.

Shadow Box

A shallow "case" designed to protect an item. On scrapbook pages, a shadow box can be created with chipboard or mat board and a transparency to inset dimensional accents to protect photos or facing pages.

Shaker

Trapping tiny accents such as beads, confetti or punches beneath a transparency elevated with foam tape. Shakers can be created in shapes or placed over patterned paper or photos to create an interactive, dimensional accent.

Shrink Plastic

Plastic sheets that can be stamped, printed or written on, then trimmed and heated in the oven or with a heat gun. Images will then shrink and thicken to result in small, raised accents.

Side-Loading

Scrapbook album in which page protectors open along one side and are designed to slip over and cover completed layouts. Created for use with strap-hinge or spiral-bound books.

Slide Mount

A plastic or cardboard holder designed to frame slides. Can be used as a mini frame for a small photo or embellishment.

Solvent Ink

An opaque stamping ink that dries quickly on slick surfaces such as metal, glass, vellum or glossy paper. Requires a special cleaner to be completely removed from stamps.

Spiral Bound

Scrapbook album featuring pages connected with a metal coil. Pages must be used as layout backgrounds or overlaid with cardstock or patterned paper.

Stencil

A cardboard, plastic or metal piece featuring a cut-out shape. A stencil can be used by brushing paint or ink over it to transfer the image to a background or by decorating the stencil itself (as in the case of alphabets) as an accent.

Stickers

Glossy or matte images, alphabets or words backed with adhesive and used to adorn scrapbook pages.

Stippling

Tapping a round brush into ink or paint and tapping it onto paper or cardstock, producing a textured, mottled finish.

Stitching

Adorning a layout with machine- or hand-sewing. The process of joining two halves to form one 12" x 12" computer scan is also known as "stitching."

Strap Hinge

Scrapbook album with pages bound together with a plastic strap. In most types, the white or black pages must either be used as the layout backgrounds or covered with cardstock or patterned paper. For use with side-loading page protectors.

Stylus

A stick with a blunt, rounded ball tip used for dry-embossing or debossing.

Tags

In sizes ranging from tiny jeweler's tags to jumbo shipping tags, these can be used as backgrounds for other embellishments or as journaling, photo mats or mini-book pages, for example. Tags are available in cardstock, pre-printed, vellum, transparency or metal varieties.

Template

A stencil, available in a variety of shapes, that can be used for dry-embossing or hand-cutting. Most often constructed from brass, plastic or cardboard.

Texture Template

A large embossed plate used to add texture to paper.

Three-Ring

Scrapbook album that features three metal, often "D"-shaped rings that snap open and shut and hold top-loading page protectors.

Tigertail

A flexible, multiple-strand thread coated in plastic. Used in beading and jewelry-making.

Tiles

Acrylic, cardboard and metal tiles that can be decorated (with paints, rubber stamps or other embellishments) and used to adorn layouts.

Top-Loading

Clear page protectors designed for post-bound or three-ring albums that are open along the top, allowing layouts to be slipped in easily.

Transparency

Crystal-clear acetate that can be used as an overlay, shaker window or background. Transparencies can often withstand the heat of embossing and can also serve as a slick surface for stamping or printing. Pre-printed varieties are also available.

Twill

A small woven strip of fabric, similar to ribbon. Twill may be plain, colored or printed with words or designs.

Vellum

Thin, semi-translucent paper that can be layered, printed on, dry-embossed, crumpled or stamped. Available in many colors, and pre-printed or texturized varieties.

Vintage

Embodying the style of a past age. Vintage scrapbooking items feature old-fashioned or retro patterns and colors, and invoke a nostalgic feel.

Walnut Ink

A rich, brown liquid (sometimes created from walnut shells) that can be used to dye, stain or add a subtle color wash to paper and fabrics. Offered in crystal, liquid, spray and ink form.

Index

CREATING KEEPSAKES

WWW.CREATINGKEEPSAKES.COM